CRAFTING
Your Own
Heritage
Album

CRAFTING
Your Own
Heritage
Album

Bev Kirschner Braun

Wedding Portrait
Helen Amelia Mummert
and
Walter Efkeman
October 31, 1920

BETTERWAY BOOKS
CINCINNATI, OHIO

ABOUT THE AUTHOR

Bev Kirschner Braun lives with her husband, Dave, and two dogs in Cincinnati, Ohio. She teaches classes part-time on heritage albums and genealogy around Cincinnati.

Crafting Your Own Heritage Album. Copyright © 2000 by Bev Braun. Manufactured in China. All rights reserved. No part of this book may be reproduced in any form or by any electronic or mechanical means including information storage and retrieval systems without permission in writing from the publisher, except by a reviewer, who may quote brief passages in a review. Published by Betterway Books, an imprint of F&W Publications, Inc., 1507 Dana Avenue, Cincinnati, Ohio 45207. (800) 289-0963. First edition.

Other fine Betterway Books are available from your local bookstore, art supply store or direct from the publisher.

04 03 02 01 00   5 4 3 2 1

Library of Congress Cataloging-in-Publication Data

Braun, Bev.
    Crafting your own heritage album / by Bev Braun.
      p. cm.
    Includes index.
    ISBN 1-55870-534-1 (pbk. : alk. paper)
    1. Genealogy Miscellanea. 2. Scrapbooks I. Title
CS14.B73 2000   99-33680
929'.1–dc21   CIP

Editor: Jane Friedman
Photography: Christine Polomsky and Al Parrish
Designer: Mary Barnes Clark
Production artist: Kathy Gardner
Production coordinator: Kristen D. Heller

The form reproduced on page 112 is reprinted from *Unpuzzling Your Past Workbook*, Betterway Books (1996), with the kind permission of Emily Croom.
The family group sheet reproduced on pages 114 and 115 is reprinted by permission of the Genealogy Records Service at http://www.genrecords.com © 1998 Genealogy Records Service.

ACKNOWLEDGMENTS

My thanks to family and friends who kindly donated photographs and documents from their personal collections for this book: Jan Dufour, Pam Boedeker, Connie Williams, Phyllis Jones Holliman, Mary and Bill Braun, and Maxine Kirschner.

A special thank you goes to Jan Dufour for taking the time to review and edit the draft of the manuscript and for her wonderful friendship.

To Kayte Ghaffar for introducing me to the staff at North Light.

To Greg Albert and Jane Friedman at North Light for their guidance and support.

To Connie Williams of Stamp Your Art Out in Cincinnati for providing an opportunity to share my love of genealogy and creating heritage albums with others.

To Pam Boedeker, an instructor at Scraps, Etc. in Cincinnati, for sharing her interest in heritage albums and scrapbook making with the rest of us.

And to my husband, Dave, for all his love and encouragement through the years.

DEDICATION

In memory of my father, John Nicholas,
and my mother, Maxine Millennor Kirschner

CHAPTER 4

JOURNALING

CHAPTER 5

GENEALOGY BASICS

⬚ Introduction ⬚

As we grow older and become wise and wonderful people, we hope that we will be remembered for something positive and worthwhile we did during our lifetimes. It doesn't have to be profound or substantial, but we hope it is significant and meaningful to at least those closest to us. Creating a family legacy that becomes a source of historical reference for current and future generations is one way of achieving that. Making a heritage album is probably one of the most rewarding projects you will ever work on. If you take the time to plan and organize what you want to accomplish, this will be an undertaking you will enjoy throughout the life of the project.

I have been actively researching and documenting my family history for over thirteen years. I have stacks of documents, photographs and memorabilia that I accumulated over that time. When I decided to begin work on my own heritage album a few years ago, I was concerned about its longevity. Scrapbooks that I created over twenty years ago are now in a state of deterioration. I started researching archival products and preservation techniques. I wanted to be sure that the products I used were safe and permanent. Much of the information in this book is a result of that research. My knowledge came from various books, magazine articles, scrapbook and genealogy classes, workshops and seminars, and research on the Internet. The resources have been too numerous to recall individually here. I am grateful to all the people who have taken the time to share their knowledge and experiences on the subjects of photo and document preservation and restoration, scrapbook making, genealogy, family history and, specifically, creating a heritage album.

The information currently available on these albums is usually a topic under scrapbooking. There are few books and magazines geared specifically to creating a heritage album. There is, however, a lot of information available at the library and bookstores to teach you the basics of scrapbook making. You will use many scrapbook techniques and supplies in your album. However, there are some key differences between the look and the content of a heritage album and that of a scrapbook or memory album.

Scrapbooks are a way to display your photographs in a more friendly and fun way than just placing them in a photo album. Memory albums are usually created to commemorate one special person or event, such as a wedding, a birth, a special vacation or attaining a major milestone. With both scrapbooks and memory albums, you can use just about any acid-free paper or embellishment to make your pages vibrant and fun. You start with bright papers, stickers, die-cuts, and then add some journaling. All this makes it more fun to look at than just flipping through the plain pages in photo albums of years past.

A heritage album, however, is an excellent way of documenting and preserving your family history. The album should include photographs, genealogical documents and well-researched and documented facts about your family history. It should include stories about family traditions, anecdotes, special memories, everyday occurrences and historical events as they relate to the lives of ancestors. It will provide a lasting bond between the past and the future. Memories, traditions and little-known facts about family and friends are recorded in the album and would be lost to future generations if not recorded.

Taking the time to preserve our photographs, documents, memorabilia and memories can fulfill the genuine need for our sense of personal and family identity and permanence. As our family members grow older, we suddenly realize the importance of documenting their memories of a passing lifestyle and era. We imagine we will always remember those things that now seem most important to us, but oral histories are not sufficient. Memories are delicate and can be fleeting. Our minds are cluttered and temperamental. These lifelong remembrances should be considered one of our most priceless possessions and recorded as soon as possible.

As you create your album, you will be researching and documenting your family history. The information you include should be thoroughly researched and verified so it is accurate, organized and presented in an attractive and elegant manner. You need to use archival-quality supplies to ensure your heritage album will not deteriorate over time like the ones put together fifty years ago.

The pages you create don't have to be perfect. They should show your creativity and should be an heirloom you are proud of. If your goal is to have all perfect pages, you may get discouraged when you make minor mistakes. With a little research and creative thinking, you'll learn little tips and tricks to help you cover these mistakes so

you won't have to redo the page. Remember, your family will be so impressed with the album you create they will never spot the mistakes. Don't be eager to point them out to anyone.

As I worked on this project, I realized that I needed to be very organized. As family members looked at the pages I created, they shared even more information and photographs with me. It is easy to let the filing and organization of this information get out of control. Take the time throughout your project to keep your information organized. If you don't, you will spend more time looking for an item than you do actually creating pages for your album.

What this book is

This book is intended to help you create a documented and well-researched, priceless family heirloom. The book will help you understand the importance of using archival-quality supplies so your album will withstand the test of time in its design and last for generations to come. These pages give you guidance on safe storage options and discuss a few of the many products now on the market to help you care for and preserve your photographs, memorabilia and documents.

This is not a step-by-step project book, but it is a guidebook that will lead you through the process of

creating a heritage album while exploring your personal creativity. It is meant to help you produce a family heirloom that not only documents a pictorial family history but also reflects your individual personality.

Who this book is for

This book is for the scrapbook maker who has created scrapbooks and memory albums in the past. If you now want to take the time to research, document and record genealogical and historical facts to go along with the photographs and journaling relating to your family and ancestors, this book will show you the right acid-free materials to use and the first steps in genealogical research.

This book is for the genealogist who has collected lots of family history information that goes beyond just names, dates and places. If you now want to create an album that includes those photographs, documents and memorabilia, this book offers guidance on making your heritage album attractive and timeless. It will help bring out your creativity and will encourage you to create an album that will become the legacy you will endow to future generations of your family.

This book can be used as a guide for teachers to help others learn and understand the importance of documenting all aspects of family history and know the personal fulfillment of creating heirloom albums for themselves and their families.

And finally, this book is for those of you who do not necessarily fall into any one of the above categories, but who have the desire to create archival-quality treasures of your own that will withstand the test of time in their beauty and elegance. I hope this book gives you the inspiration and information you need to do just that! Enjoy!

Twelfth Day.

HASE back the shadows,
      gray and old,
Of the dead ages, from his way,
And let his hopeful eyes
            behold
The dawn of Thy millenial day.

Lines.

he wrongs of man to man ... make
            The love of ...
As through the shadow ... plain,
      The eye loo...
On gleams of sta...
The glaring sunshine...

Then let us ...
      And he...
There's life alone...

Thirteenth Day.

Youthful years and maiden beauty,
Joy with them should still abide—
            Instinct take the
      place of
            Duty—
      Love, not Reason
            guide.

      Ever in the
      New rejoicing,
Kindly beckoning
            back the
                  Old,
Turning with a
      power like Midas
All things into
      gold.

To —

Original Copy

Certifica

CHAPTER 1
Getting Started

The first step in creating your heritage album is to gather your photographs, memorabilia and documents. Look everywhere for things to put in your album. Look in old photo albums, closets, dresser drawers, the attic, the basement and the garage. Look at pictures and anything else that might already be framed. Talk to your family, especially the older members; they may have bits and pieces of information that will help you on your way.

ORGANIZING YOUR COLLECTION

You'll need to get organized just like you would for any other project. Like most of us, you probably have a large box of pictures, documents and memorabilia that needs to be sorted into some kind of order.

The way in which you organize your massive assortment isn't that important. What really matters is that you put your collection into some kind of workable order. You want to be able to easily retrieve information about a particular person or family when you are ready to work on that section of your album.

The whole point of being organized is being able to find things quickly and easily. You will save yourself a lot of time looking for things if you get organized from the beginning of this project. The time you save not searching for items can be spent actually creating your album pages. As you work on your album, take the time to get reorganized whenever things start getting mixed together or pulled out of order. Re-sort and refile often so you will continue to enjoy your activity.

Get your treasured family history organized before it is lost forever!

SORTING OPTIONS

The three simplest ways to organize your collection are chronologically (by years or decades), by families and by each individual person. Use rubber bands and blank file cards, or start with a package of large manila envelopes available from any discount or office supply store. You can label each card or envelope with one of the sorting options below.

CHRONOLOGICALLY

Sorting everything chronologically can be an easy way to get started. Depending on how much historical information and how many pictures you have, you can sort by decades (1951–1960, 1961–1970), by half centuries (1950–2000, 1900–1949) or by centuries (1700, 1800, 1900). Once you get things sorted into stacks, you can always go back and sort them into smaller stacks after you decide exactly how you are going to organize your album.

BY FAMILY

If you are working on both lines of your family as well as your spouse's, you can begin with four major stacks or packets of information—one stack each for your mother and father, and one stack each for your spouse's mother and father.

BY INDIVIDUAL

If you have mounds of information like I do, one of the easiest ways to get started is to sort and place all of your

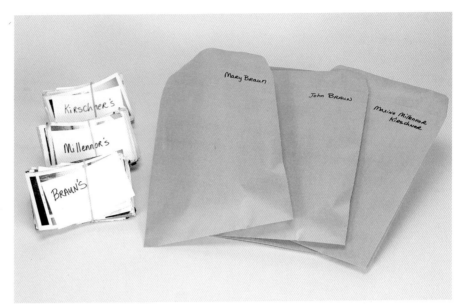

Organizing photographs into stacks by "family" name or in envelopes by "individuals" are two quick and simple ways to get started sorting your collection.

photographs, documents, memorabilia and stories relating to one person inside a large envelope. Write the person's name on the outside of the envelope, and place everything you find pertaining to that person in that envelope. When you get ready to work on that person in your album, everything will be together.

If you have a picture or document that fits in with several different families, you may not know how or where you will use it. Take another large manila envelope and write the family name on it. Put items in it that need to be looked at further when you get ready to add things to your album that include members of that family.

If you have any oral histories either on tape or written, be sure to keep them with the rest of the person's history so you can use them when you get ready to do your journaling.

ITEMS TO INCLUDE

You will have many items as you sort through your collection. You want to ensure a well-documented history of each person or family in the "chapters" of your album. Some items to include are listed below.

What to Include in Your Heritage Album

- pictures of primary family members with names and relationships to you

- graphical representation of immediate family members

- copies of official documents (birth, death, baptismal and marriage certificates; naturalization papers; land deeds)

- information about primary person's spouse and primary family members (parents, siblings, children)

- time lines of major known facts about the family (employment history, residences, births, deaths, marriages)

- personal histories about family provided by oral histories, family members, family traditions, anecdotes, historical documents

- mementos to be shared with future generations (war medals and military dog tags, hospital birth bracelets, picture locket, hobby samples, locks of hair)

- brief recap of significant historical, social or political events that affected the lives of a particular family you are documenting

- information about family hobbies or special talents

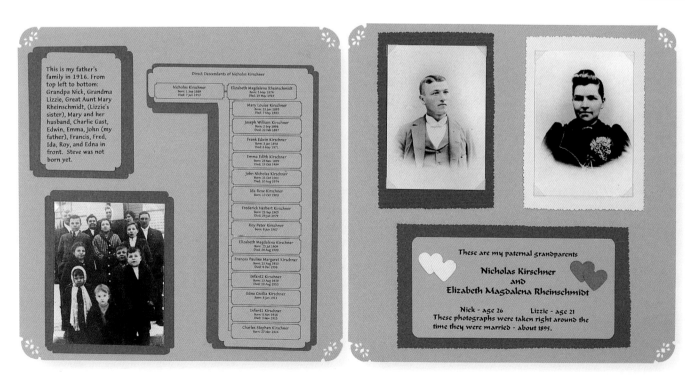

A descendent chart is an easy way to show family relationships, especially if you have a photo of your ancestors to go with it.

Death Certificate for John Nicholas Kirschner
October 31, 1901 - August 10, 1974

Source: Clermont County General Health District Office
Environmental Division 2275 Bauer Road Batavia, Ohio

Death Certificate for John Nicholas Kirschner
October 31, 1901 - August 10, 1974
Above is the backside of the death certificate
Source: Clermont County General Health District Office
Environmental Division 2275 Bauer Road Batavia, Ohio

Birth Certificate for John Nicholas Kirschner
October 31, 1901

Source: Brown County, Union Township, Ohio
Probate Court Records, Georgetown, Ohio
Birth Records Volume 3, page 232

Official genealogical documents, along with pictures and journaling, are a great
way to showcase an individual family member.

Time lines can show a snapshot of significant events in the lives of your ancestors.

ITEMS TO SAVE

There are many items you can save for your album. You can collect anything that will give meaning and purpose to your album by helping to explain what was going on in a particular person's life at a specific time in history. The list on the right mentions a few examples.

A primary reason for creating a heritage album is to tell the story of your ancestors' life histories. A heritage album should include all of the good things that occur in a family's life, as well as the not-so-good. It is important for your present family members, as well as future generations, to know where family members have been and what they went through. This will give your family a much richer understanding of why things are the way they are now.

What to Save

• Newspaper articles about family members or close friends

• Diplomas, certificates of achievement, report cards, school transcripts

• Invitations, announcements (birth, engagement, wedding, graduation)

• Family tree information

• Death information (obituaries, prayer cards, sympathy cards)

Collecting and saving pieces of your family history help tell the story of your heritage through documentation of the events in people's lives.

WHAT'S MISSING?

As you sort through your collection and review the previous list of items to include, you may find you are missing information and documents that will validate your family's heritage. In chapter five, we'll discuss genealogical research and some of the places you can look to help locate some of the missing information.

But you don't need to wait until you have all of the information before you start on your album. As you lay out your pages, you may not be able to complete every page before you move on to the next. If you are not sure of all the names of everyone in a photograph or how old someone is, do a page mock-up until you have more complete and accurate information.

Dave's Maternal Great-Great
Grandparents
Mr. & Mrs. Finke
St. Bernard, Ohio

Dave's Maternal Great Grandparents
Mary Amelia Finke
and
Albert Joseph Mummert
Abt. 1891

Use plain white paper with a draft of the journaling to do mock-ups. Attach them to the page with acid-free temporary adhesive tape until your research is complete. Add journaling with accurate information in the final format.

ARCHIVAL INFORMATION

A heritage album will take a lot of your time and energy to create and assemble. You'll want to be confident that it will last as long as possible and look great for the next few hundred years. You won't want it to start deteriorating in twenty to thirty years. To ensure that it doesn't, use only 100 percent archival-safe materials. You are creating a priceless heirloom for future generations and do not want to worry about its longevity.

Archival Terminology

Acid-free
Materials that have a pH of 7.0 or higher. This term indicates the absence of acid. It is important to use acid-free products since acid breaks down paper and photographs. This term is sometimes used incorrectly as a synonym for alkaline or buffered.

Acid migration
The transfer of acid from an acidic material to a less acidic material or pH-neutral material. Acid always migrates to neutral, never the other way around.

Archival quality
Indicates a material or product is permanent, durable or chemically stable, and that it can, therefore, safely be used for preservation.

Buffered paper
A paper that is pH neutral to begin with and has been made more alkaline to neutralize additional acids that may migrate to the paper.

Lignin
A chemical compound largely responsible for the strength and rigidity of plants. Its presence in paper is believed to contribute to chemical deterioration. Paper with less than one percent lignin is considered lignin-free. Lignin is believed to be more harmful to photographs than acid.

Mylar (polyester, polypropylene)
Used as a protective clear covering for photos and album pages. Mylar is currently regarded as the highest quality material used for this purpose.

Photo safe
A term loosely used by many companies to indicate that they believe their products are safe to use with photographs. There is no regulation of the term by a legally enforceable standard. This term is used in many instances when a product is not, in fact, safe to be used near photos. Inaccurate use of this term may be due to ignorance, a wish to deceive or just a lack of photo preservation knowledge.

Polyvinyl chloride (PVC)
A material found in some plastic products and adhesives that can break down to form acids.

Paper deterioration

Color photographs, documents, newsprint and books printed on paper are prone to deterioration. The primary cause is from the acid in poor-quality papers. The poorest quality of paper is usually newsprint and tends to be the first to decay. It will turn brown and brittle. Another problem that causes deterioration is acid migration, which is when low-quality paper tends to bleed onto neighboring pieces of paper. You may have seen an old document that had a newspaper clipping enclosed with it for many years. The document may have brown stains on it caused by the acid migration, which also shortens the life span of the document's paper.

With some papers, such as newspaper clippings, the best solution is to photocopy this information on acid-free buffered paper. Place the photocopy in your album. The original documents and newspaper clippings may continue to deteriorate, so you may want to store them in an acid-free page protector (discussed later in this chapter).

There are products available that allow you to remove most of the acid content of paper and newsprint. You spray both sides of the document or newspaper item with products such as Wei T'O Associates' Good News line and Preservation Technologies' new Archival Mist deacidification sprays and solutions. These products help protect paper against yellowing, deterioration and crumbling for hundreds of years. You can then place the treated newsprint or document in your album on buffered paper to reduce further acid migration.

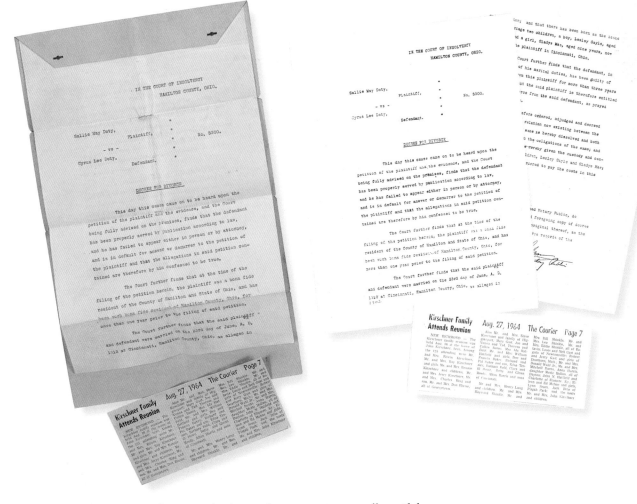

Photocopies are an easy solution to displaying documents in your album if the original paper is deteriorating.

PAPER STORAGE AND PRESERVATION

Proper storage is important to preserving your family documents, and it can increase the life span of any piece of paper. Light, humidity, heat and improper handling of paper by people cause the most damage to a paper's life span.

The old letters, written documents, photographs and newspaper clippings should be stored safely until they are placed in your album. This will help ensure that they do not suffer any additional decay or damage.

One stable storage option for a document or newspaper is to place it between two pieces of acid-free buffered paper and then place it in a plastic sheet protector. Then it can be safely stored in a bank safety-deposit box or in an air-conditioned closet of your house. The buffered paper can be changed periodically if acid migration occurs.

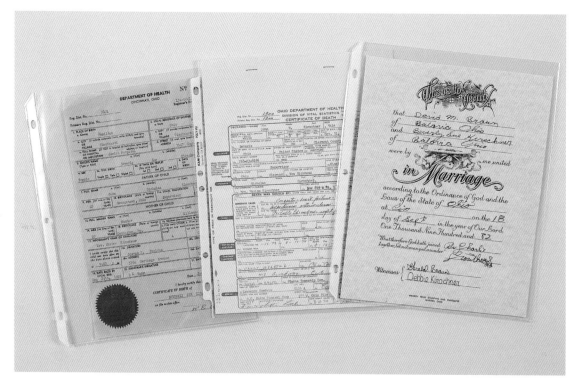

Using archival-quality, top-loading sheet protectors to protect your original documents is an easy storage solution.

Tips on Paper Storage

- Store papers opened and flat (not folded) in archival-safe sheet protectors, or place a document between two pieces of blank archival-safe paper, which can then be replaced if acid migration occurs.

- Place paper items in acid-free page protectors to prevent them from rubbing against each other and causing further deterioration.

- Don't hang one-of-a-kind documents in direct sunlight. They will quickly fade and deteriorate.

- Don't use self-adhesive tapes or glue to repair torn paper or bookbindings. In the long run it will cause more damage to the paper. There are acid-free adhesive tapes that you can use on the backs of photographs to repair them.

- Don't laminate family heirlooms and one-of-a kind documents. This will not prolong the life of the paper and cannot be undone.

- Don't use staples, paper clips or other metal objects with paper, as they will eventually rust.

- Don't store documents or photographs in attics (usually hot and humid) or in basements (usually damp). They should be stored in a cool, dry place.

Repair of this photo was attempted with regular adhesive tape years ago. It has come loose and turned yellow as it deteriorated. Use only archival adhesive tapes if you decide to repair a photo or document on your own.

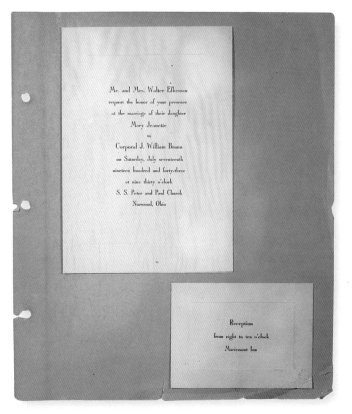

The brown stains on the wedding invitation and announcement card are from acid migration. The photo album page is over fifty years old, and the papers were not acid-free.

PHOTOGRAPH PRESERVATION

There are several factors that can cause deterioration problems for photographs. These are the same conditions that cause paper deterioration: humidity, sunlight, dirt, dust and fingerprints. Inadequate processing can cause photos to become discolored or fade over time.

An inexpensive option I use most is to make photocopies of old photographs on acid-free paper. This is an economical way to make good-quality copies of just the photos you want to use in your album. You can make beautiful copies of black-and-white photos on a color copy machine by setting it on the black-and-white setting. Put the copy in your album, and store the original photograph using one of the safe storage methods mentioned later in this chapter.

Another option is to use the Kodak Picture Maker systems available in many chain department or discount stores to make copies and enlargements of photos without negatives. You can make duplicate photographs in different sizes from wallet size to 8" x 10", and many systems offer other features to enhance pictures as they are being made. Using these systems, you can intensify the photo's color if it has faded, zoom in, crop out unwanted background items and eliminate red-eye.

Sisters and Brothers of Amelia Finke Mummert - Dave Braun's Great Grandmother
(Mother of Helen Mummert Efkeman)

Front Row: Uncle Johnny Finke (Brother)   Aunt Gertrude Hoffman

Second Row: Aunt Ann Daly (Sister)   Uncle Henry Lauman Aunt Elizabeth Lauman(Liza) (Sister)

Third Row: Aunt Mary Finke   Uncle Ben Finke (Brother) Grandma Amelia Finke Mummert
Aunt Mary (Sister-in-law married to Dan Finke) Uncle John Schaefer Aunt Cecilia Mummert Schaefer (Sister)

Family: Brothers: Dan, Ben, John   Sisters: Amelia, Ann, Elizabeth, Cecilia

This slightly damaged family photograph photocopied beautifully on a color photocopy machine.

PHOTOGRAPH RESTORATION

There are several physical and chemical treatments that can be used to improve the aesthetics and physical strength of an old photograph. When considering any type of restoration to an original photograph, you need to be aware that there is a risk of additional harm being done

If the photograph to be repaired or restored is a one-of-a-kind photograph and it has been damaged, don't attempt to make any repairs to the photo yourself. Take the photograph to a qualified photo conservator. This can be an expensive process, sometimes ranging from $50 to as much as $250, but the results will be worth it if it is done right. You might not want to spend this much money to repair a photograph for your album. You could get the photograph restored and display it in an archival-safe frame. Make an inexpensive copy of the repaired photo for your album.

There are several types of photographic restoration that can be done, and I'll cover just a few briefly. If you decide to have restoration work done, do your research so you understand exactly what is involved in each of the following processes and others that are available.

DIGITAL OR ELECTRONIC IMAGING

This restoration begins with the photograph being scanned. A digital version of the photograph is electronically projected onto a computer screen. A skilled artist uses an electronic device that looks like a ball-point pen to restore the color and quality of the original photograph. The quality of the finished product depends upon how damaged the photograph was to begin with. The cost of

this procedure can be between $50 and $150 for an 8" x 10" photograph.

CHEMICAL RESTORATION OF BLACK-AND-WHITE PHOTOGRAPHS

There are two processes for chemically restoring black-and-white photographs. The original photograph can be redeveloped in a black-and-white developer or it can be bleached and redeveloped. Because both of these processes involve irreversible changes to the original photograph, only a photographic conservator should be allowed to do this work.

AIRBRUSH RESTORATION

Airbrush restoration involves a skilled artist and a paintbrush that "atomizes" the paint. A copy of the print is made, and all work is done on the copy. There are a lot of steps and details involved in the process. Almost anything can be achieved with airbrush restoration if the artist is well qualified. However, the more airbrush work that is done to a photograph, the less the finished piece is going to look like a photograph.

COPYING

This process involves having a copy negative made of an original photograph and having additional copies made. Corrections can be made to the negative during the duplication process to improve the quality of the finished photograph. You can also request archival finishing for the copy negative and print from a quality photographic lab to add to the photo's

long-term stability. Copying allows you to produce reprints in quantities and provides you with protection for your precious family photographs so they won't deteriorate and be lost forever.

PHOTOGRAPH STORAGE

Don't store photographs in magnetic photo albums. Even the newer ones that say "photo safe" need to be checked with the manufacturer. Put your photographs in archival-safe plastic sleeves, and store them in three-ring binders. This will protect your photographs from rubbing against each other or from being crushed.

If you have shoebox-type photo boxes and you're not sure they are acid-free, line the inside with acid-free buffered paper. You should change the buffered paper periodically to ensure that any acid migration from the box to the paper does not harm your photographs. If you make your own dividers for your photo boxes, use acid-free buffered cardstock.

The Highsmith Photo Chest and Photo Tote units are low-cost, acid-free (neutral pH) corruboard storage units.

Photo sleeves come in a variety of sizes and are a great way to store and protect photographs in three-ring binders. Larger photos can be stored in top-loading sheet protectors.

CRAFTING YOUR OWN HERITAGE ALBUM

LABELING PHOTOGRAPHS

As you sort your photographs for storage, use a photographic marker to note details on the back of each photograph. This will not damage them or bleed through to the front like a ballpoint pen will. These markers are inexpensive and are available at photography and craft stores or by mail order from scrapbook and photography suppliers.

It may be a few days or a few years before you are ready to put the photos in your album. Don't rely on your memory. If you have special memories you want to record in your album with a photograph, write notes on a separate piece of paper and keep it with the photo. You can use this information as part of your journaling when you are putting the photograph on a page of your album.

STORING NEGATIVES

Negatives need to be organized and stored with just as much care as your photographs. The sleeves that your negatives are returned in from the photo lab are not always photo safe. Put your negatives in archival-quality plastic sleeves and store them in three-ring binders. Label your negative sleeves so you can easily find the right negative if you need to make copies.

Warning! Do not store your negatives and photographs together. I suggest keeping the negatives in a bank safety-deposit box or at someone else's house. If a disaster takes place, such as a fire, flood or tornado, and your photographs are lost, you will still have the negatives if they are stored in a separate place.

The best way to store negatives is in archival quality plastic sleeves that can be purchased at any photography supply store.

CHAPTER 2

The Album

Choosing an album is a personal choice. Look at different album types, and select the one that best suits the project you are working on. Decide how you will store and display your album. This will help determine whether you choose an album that needs to lie flat when it is open or stand upright on a bookcase shelf.

When selecting an album, be sure you can move the pages easily without affecting other pages. You will want to expand and add new pages as you find more photographs, documents and family treasures that need to be included. Also, the album should have a sturdy binding and cover if it will be handled a lot.

Album pages come in different sizes. If you have trouble deciding what size pages to use, try the same layout on two different sizes. See which one works best for you before making your final album selection.

ALBUM CHOICES

THREE-RING BINDERS

The least expensive choice is the three-ring binder. It is very versatile, and easy to use. D-ring binders allow pages to stay flat, and O-ring binders make page turning easier. The larger binder rings allow more pages to be put into them.

Pages are stored in acid-free page protectors, so the binder needs to be oversized to accommodate these. Each sheet protector represents one page and should contain two pieces of individual cardstock back-to-back. Use only one side of the cardstock so you can easily move pages without affecting others.

With a three-ring binder, a two-page spread will have binder rings between the pages when the album is opened for display, which you may not like. Pages can also slip out of the top-loading page protectors if the book is dropped or turned upside down.

STRAP-BOUND EXPANDABLE ALBUMS

A strap-bound expandable album has a plastic strap binding that allows your album to expand. Facing pages lie flat and flush side by side when the album is open without any binding showing in the middle. The albums have one-color background pages (usually white). Pages can be moved; however, if you use both sides of each page, it is more difficult to move the pages and keep the heritage information in order. Some of these albums have reinforced edges to help protect against wear and tear. Page protectors are available for these album pages if the pages are bound into the straps. Some strap-bound albums have the page protectors bound in with straps, and the pages slip into the top of the protector.

POST-BOUND ALBUMS

Post-bound albums are hole-punched pages with metal posts and are expandable by adding post extensions. Sheet protectors for this type of album are also available. There are different colors of background pages, including black, white and cream. Two-page displays are side by side but pages do not lie totally flat when the album is open. If you move a page, you are affecting both sides of the page.

Three-ring binders expand and pages are easily moved around.

Strap-bound expandable albums allow for any number of photographs and documents.

Post-bound scrapbooks are large, and the pages can be rearranged.

SPIRAL-BOUND ALBUMS

Spiral binders are good for single-theme scrapbooks, such as a brag book. You will be placing photos and documents on both sides of the paper, so the rings must be large to accommodate the additional thickness. You cannot add or move pages in spiral binders so they are limiting.

Spiral binders would not be a good choice for a heritage album. Page protectors are not available for these albums.

MAGNETIC PHOTO ALBUMS

I recommend that you don't use "magnetic" page albums. Your photographs and documents will most likely deteriorate faster in them. Most of the damage to your photos and documents occurs in the first five years they are in magnetic albums. If you have photos currently stored in a magnetic photo album, take your pictures out of it so they won't deteriorate any further. Store these photographs in a photo-safe storage box or in photo sleeves until you are ready to put them in an archival-safe photo album.

Magnetic photo albums that are found in most stores today should not be used for your photographs or documents. Even if they say "photo safe," they may not be.

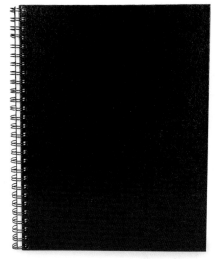

To prevent further deterioration of your photos, remove them from magnetic photo albums. Slide dental floss behind a picture to lift it off the page.

Spiral-bound albums expand, but pages cannot be rearranged.

If you have trouble getting photos off magnetic album pages, use acid-free Un-Du to remove any adhesive. The solution instantly neutralizes the adhesive temporarily and then quickly evaporates allowing you to reuse the item. It also works well on photo corners, die-cuts, stickers and postage stamps.

ALBUM PAGE SIZES

The two most popular sizes for album pages are 8½"x11" and 12"x12". Both sizes have pros and cons.

8½"x11" page		12"x12" page	
Pro	Con	Pro	Con
This page will feed through most printers if you want to use computer fonts and clip art. Photocopying is less expensive if you want to share your album pages with others.	The space is more limiting so you have less room for layouts. You can only place one to two pictures and some journaling in this space.	This size gives more room for layouts of pictures and journaling without looking crowded. You can put three to five photographs and journaling on one page.	Larger-size papers won't feed through most copiers and home printers. Photocopies are more expensive if you want to share your pages with others.

These two pages have essentially the same photographs and journaling on them. The middle photograph on the 8½"x11" layout was cropped and the journaling font was reduced to fit on the smaller page. The 12"x12" layout looks less crowded and has a little more white space showing.

SHEET PROTECTORS

Sheet protectors enclose the album pages and keep photographs on facing pages from rubbing together. Top-loading sheet protectors are the most frequently used. Side loaders open on the left and can keep your pages from falling out if the album is dropped or turned upside down. Sheet protectors come in standard and heavyweight strengths. The heavyweight versions cost a little more, but they will provide extra support to your pages. Archival-safe sheet protectors are available at office supply and scrapbook supply stores. Use them in a separate three-ring binder to store documents and larger photographs, or in your album to cover pages.

Archival-safe sheet protectors used with three-ring binders will hold your scrapbook pages and protect them from oily fingerprints, dirt, dust and spills. They are sealed on three sides, and the cardstock slides in from the top or one side.

BASIC SUPPLIES

Don't buy too many scrapbooking supplies when you first get started. You will become overwhelmed, and it will be more difficult to stay organized. Once you develop your own style, you can add to your supplies inventory. Here is a list of the basic supplies you need to get started on your album pages.

Basic Tools to Get You Started

- photo-safe adhesives (photo corners, photo sticker squares)

- black medium-tip permanent pen

- sharp, straight scissors

- decorative scissors

- corner rounder punch, decorative corner punch, maybe a photo slit punch

- archival-safe album or three-ring binder

- polypropylene sheet protectors (8½"x11" or 12"x12")

- heavy weight, acid-free, lignin-free, buffered paper

- 12-inch personal paper trimmers

- pH testing pen (to test paper products for acid content)

- photographic marker (for writing information on back of photos)

- ruler

CRAFTING YOUR OWN HERITAGE ALBUM

How to use your tools

Add a touch of elegance to the corners of your album pages using decorative corner punches and simple corner rounder punches.

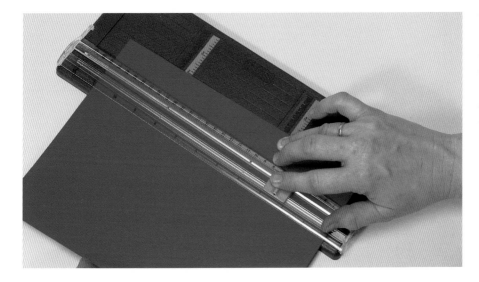

Fiskars personal paper trimmer gives accurate straight-cut edges. It lies flat on the table, trims paper up to 12 inches and includes a swing-arm ruler. The trimmer cuts two layers of cardstock at once and is great for cropping photographs.

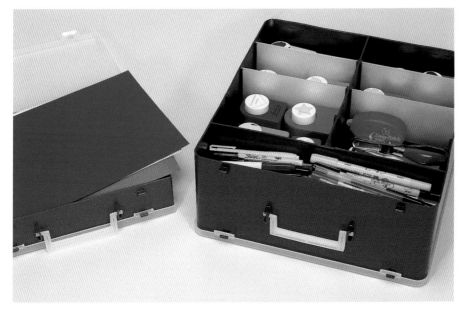

Cropper Hopper dual-sided scrapbook supply and paper cases are available in 8½"x11" and 12"x12" to help you organize and easily store your supplies.

CHAPTER 3
Album Assembly

Developing a style or consistent design format throughout your album will add to its overall beauty. It will also tie all of the elements together—photographs, mementos and journaling. There are endless options and possibilities for creating page consistencies and "templates." You can use the same colors of paper throughout, the same basic layout on each page or the same border. Other ways to create unity include using the same die-cut, verse or rubber stamp design in the corner of each page. If you don't know what you want to do throughout your album, you can always add something later if you allow room on your pages.

SELECTING PAPERS

There is a wide variety of plain and patterned acid-free papers to choose from. Both are available in 8½"x11" and 12"x12". Papers come in different weights from stationery at 20-lb. weight to heavier 80-lb. weight cardstock. The heavier papers are usually best for your background papers. If you choose to mat your photographs and documents, you can use the lighter-weight papers and then adhere them to the background paper.

COLOR

Color is important to the overall elegance and timelessness of your album. Paper colors in a heritage album are generally soft, classic colors (moss and hunter green, peach, rose, mauve, burgundy, black, gray, cream, dark purple and lilac) rather than bold and bright. There are wonderful printed papers available.

There may be instances when you have a color photograph that looks best using a bolder color mat or background page. Use the color that conveys the best mood for that page, but remember to keep the style and theme of your heritage album consistent.

Narrowing the variety of paper colors to four to six can create a continuity that ties everything together. It will give the album organization and elegance. It will also make your layout choices easier and faster by not having to select from an array of color combinations.

Different background colors will bring out different tones and highlights in a photograph, document or memento. Try several different colors of paper until you find the one that best complements the focal point of your photographs.

Organizing your Heritage Album

You need to decide how you want to organize your album. You can organize it by family generation lines, by individual families, in chronological order or by major events. Whatever your decision, allow for modifications and flexibility. You may want to move things around later. Or, you may find or be given more photographs, documents or memorabilia during the process that you want to add.

TITLE PAGE

If you haven't decided whether or not to create a customized cover for your album, you can create a title page that includes information about your album. This should be the first page and reinforce the theme of your album with information such as "Smith Family—Five Generations" or "The John Smith Family Heritage Album" or "Fifty Years of Smith Family Weddings."

KIRSCHNER
HERITAGE ALBUM
VOLUME 1

Direct Descendants of Herbert Kirschner

Herbert Kirschner
Born: 16 Mar 1827
Died: 7 Oct 1908

Clara Eva Huber
Born: 24 Mar 1830
Died: 8 Aug 1921

Nicholas Kirschner
Born: 1 Sep 1869
Died: 7 Jun 1953

Elizabeth Magdalena
Rheinschmidt
Born: 5 May 1874
Died: 19 May 1919

John Nicholas Kirschner
Born: 31 Oct 1901
Died: 10 Aug 1974

Florence Maxine Millennor
Born: 23 Oct 1925

Beverly Sue Kirschner
Born: 6 Dec 1952

created by: Bev Kirschner Braun - 1999

Title pages are an excellent way of identifying the contents of your heritage album or a specific chapter in it.

Weave a garland border around a title page for an elegant touch.

WORK IN MANAGEABLE SEGMENTS

You can start anywhere and with anyone in your album as long as you have the option of moving pages or inserting new ones. If you are working with cardstock and page protectors in a three-ring binder, you work on only one side of the page. You can move these as you complete pages or find more information you want to add. If you are working on both sides of the album page, you will have to be more careful with what you place on the pages in case you want to move them.

If your album choice doesn't allow for the option of rearranging pages, you will need to be very organized. You should have almost all of your information available before you put your album pages together. Once the photographs and documents are adhered to the pages, they will have to remain in that order. You may want to make an outline of the pages in your album before completing them so you can see how the book will go together.

The outline may help you decide if you want to make changes before you start.

If you have your collection sorted and organized by families or by each individual, you are ready to begin. Start with one of those stacks or packets. Pick one person or family, and begin laying out the photographs, documents and memorabilia you have for them. Work on that person or family until you run out of materials or ideas. Then move on to another person or family.

Get started by selecting one of the packets of information you sorted on one person. Lay out the photographs and information to design your album page, and soon you'll see the results of your first pages.

CHOOSING THE BEST PHOTOGRAPHS

Sort and choose only the best photographs. You can't include every photograph you have ever taken or collected. Most of us take lots of pictures and sometimes several of them look very similar. Look over the photos carefully, and select those with the best clarity and sharpness.

Determine what you want to focus on in the picture. This will help you decide which photo to select. If the primary person or object you want to focus on is at different distances in several photographs, choose the one closest to the camera. Select only those pictures that will tell the story in the best way.

Sometimes selecting the best photograph is as simple as looking at subtle differences in the shading in black and white photos and choosing the one you like best.

In these three photographs, I decided I wanted the focus on just one person, my friend Jan. The best photograph is the one with her closest to the camera.

ORIGINALS VS. DUPLICATES

I don't recommend using one-of-a-kind photographs or original documents in a heritage album. Make color copies of photos and documents and store the originals using a safe storage option discussed in chapter one. Both black-and-white and sepia-tone photographs copy beautifully on a color copier using the black-and-white feature.

Tip

Your hands should be clean and oil-free when handling photographs and documents. Fingerprints can cause long-term damage to both.

Sallie Mae Williams Jordan and her second husband Will Jordan. This picture was taken around 1920. She is my great Aunt "Mae", my maternal grandfather's Aunt.

An inexpensive way to display photographs in your album is to make color photocopies of original photographs. The original photograph is on the right. The originals can be stored in a safe storage environment.

A color photocopy was made of this original (right) using the black-and-white setting and reducing to 50 percent of its original size.

The original photograph is on the left, the photocopy on the right.

MOUNTING ORIGINAL PHOTOGRAPHS

If you have only original photographs to use in your album, you may not want to permanently affix them to the page. You may want to make copies of the photos, and if so, you will want to easily remove them and put them back without causing damage. Using photo corners to mount your photographs is a good way to prevent trouble. They are simple to use and hold your photos securely, but may be removed. The corners come in all colors: pastels, bolds, black, gold, white and transparent. Some are self-adhesive, and others need to be moistened to activate the adhesive. I place a photo corner on each corner of the photograph and then attach the corners to the mat or album page. Other methods of mounting photos are demonstrated on this page.

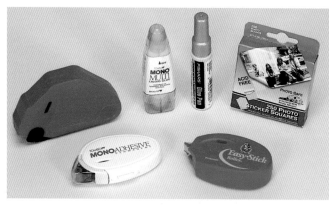

Most scrapbook makers have several kinds of adhesives on hand so they can use the one that is most appropriate for the situation.

For photos or copies you won't need to remove, use photo mounts or photo stickers. These double-sided squares are placed on the backs of your photos or documents.

Photo corners are used to mount original photographs or documents to the page so they can be easily removed later.

Photo slit punches are an easy way to elegantly display original photos and documents in your album and still be able to remove them if you want to.

CROPPING

Cropping a photograph simply means cutting a photograph to improve the focus or placing a frame around it to create a focus. Some photographs are not properly framed at the time they are taken and may need to be cropped to remove distracting background. You can mark your cropping line on photos and documents with a grease pencil and a ruler or by using a see-through plastic template. Then use a paper cutter for straight cuts or scissors for curves and cut just inside the line. Immediately wipe off the grease pencil markings.

I don't recommend cropping original photographs unless you have duplicates. Make a copy and then crop the copy rather than the original. The general rule is don't do anything to original photographs or documents that you can't undo if you don't have copies of them.

Don't crop out details in the background of your photograph that will help date it, such as the family car, a vacation house or a historic landmark. Be sure to include information about those items as you journal. This will give a more complete description of what the photograph is about and when and where it was taken.

Tip

Don't crop instant Polaroid photographs since they are one-of-a-kind photos. They also contain an acidic gel inside of them that, if cut, will bleed to other photographs.

Trimming photos or using frames can eliminate annoying details in a photo that take away from the focal point.

MATTING PHOTOGRAPHS

Your photos and documents can be directly adhered to the album pages, or you can mat them using coordinating background paper. Matting means taking a cropped photograph and adhering it to a piece of plain or patterned paper, then trimming the "mat" to about ⅛-inch away from the photograph. Learning to mat photographs and documents is a great way to bring out the colors in your photographs. You can use cardstock, patterned paper, stationery, etc. You can use a single mat or several layers, depending on the effect you want. Another way to tie family lines together in your album is by using specific colors for each generation or family line. Try different weights and colors of paper for your mats when you begin your heritage album. When you decide which you like best (one or two mats for each document and photograph), use this throughout the album to ensure consistency.

Deciding to use one or two mats behind your photographs and documents is an easy way to add an eye-catching frame. Try contrasting colors, patterned paper and layering with different thicknesses of paper to see what looks best.

LAYOUTS

A layout is the way your photographs, documents, journaling, die-cuts, etc., are arranged on the page. Each page should have a focal point. Decide what you want to stand out on the page and then arrange other items around it. You can place the photograph at an angle to focus attention on it. In most scrapbooks you will be looking at two pages at once. Sometimes the information you have is only enough to make a one-page layout. It is a good idea to have continuity on

the two facing pages by using coordinating paper and the same type of journaling on both. Some layouts will need two or more pages to tell the best story, so don't limit yourself to one page.

Look through scrapbook and craft magazines to see some of the ideas that others have used to design their pages. These publications are available at public libraries and places where craft magazines are sold. There are also lots of ideas available on the Internet

(check the resource guide in the back of this book for magazine and Web site information).

Pages should not be cluttered. Don't feel as if you have to fill all the space on an album page. Sometimes less is better and simple layouts are more elegant and tasteful. Leave plenty of space to add journaling (chapter four) on each page to bring the photos and documents to life.

Simple color can showcase and enhance the beauty of a photograph. Look at the dramatic difference between the black-and-white photo used with blue and black papers, and the sepia photo used with the cream and brown paper. Both layouts are simple but elegant.

TEMPLATES

Using templates, or stencils, can make creating page layouts easy and fun. There is a wide variety of template shapes and sizes to select from (hearts, squares, circles, holiday designs, alphabet, borders, etc.) depending upon the type of page you want to create. Templates are simple tools that can help you crop photos, create shapes and add lettering and borders to your pages quickly and accurately.

You can purchase templates or make your own. Purchased templates are usually thin sheets of hard plastic with different shapes cut out of them. You can make your own templates out of cardboard or a file folder. Trace the shapes on the cardboard and then use a craft knife to cut out each shape. By making your own, you can customize your templates with just the shapes you want to use throughout your album.

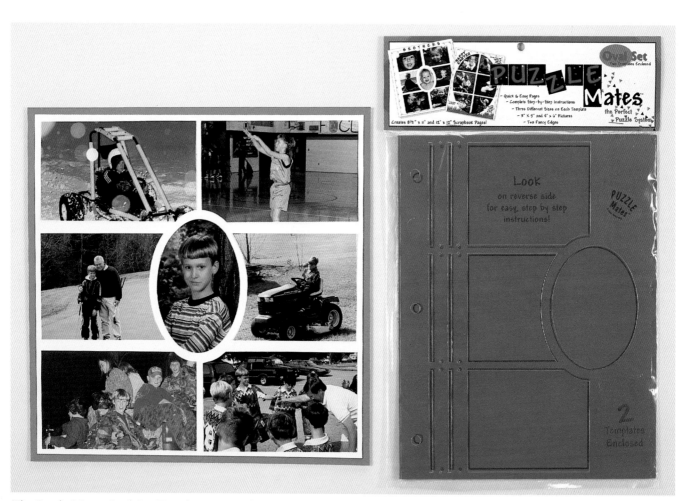

The Puzzle Mates Oval Set Template was used to create this collage. Puzzle Mates come in a variety of shapes, and each set includes step-by-step instructions, three different sizes on each template and two fancy edges for creating 8½"x11" or 12"x12" pages.

PANORAMIC PAGES

Some stories can't be told in just one or two pages. Panoramic page protectors from Frances Meyer, Inc. are a great way of telling the whole story. Use one set in a three-ring binder and open it to show four full pages at a time.

BORDERS

When you are designing a page layout, decide whether you want to use a border. A simple border can add some color and enhancement to a page. Most borders are fast and easy to create and take up only a little page space, leaving lots of room for photographs and journaling.

The type of border you use will determine how much space you have remaining for the rest of the layout. You can use plain or decorative paper, fancy scissors, paper punches, fancy rulers and pens, stickers and clip art. As you look at the page layouts throughout this book, you'll see many examples of borders that you can copy.

4th of July 1962 Millennor Family at the farm on Ten Mile Road near Amelia, Ohio

Above: Mom (Maxine) with her parents, Marie and Warren Millennor, Aunt Mae Jordan in background, & Lassie, the dog

Above Right: Aunt Nannie, and Grandpa Warren in front, Aunt Eva and Aunt Mae in back.

Right: Front - Aunt Nannie, Aunt Mae Jordan, Grandpa Warren, in back - Uncle Barnes, Grandma Marie, and Aunt Eva

Corner Genie templates were used to create these borders to add a touch of beauty and simplicity to the page layouts.

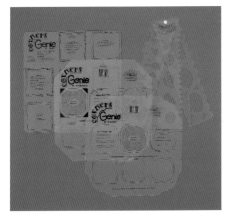

Corner Genie templates from Chatterbox: Each set contains two templates that let you draw straight and evenly spaced lines around the edges of your pages to create fast and easy borders for 12"x12" pages.

Rule-It-Up rulers from Cut-It-Up can be used for creating borders and die-cut shapes on your album pages.

Fiskars and Olfa rotary paper cutters are used with a self-healing cutting mat to make straight cuts and square corners. Use fancy cutting blades to make these effortless borders.

Simple borders can be made with rotary cutters and coordinating paper.

EMBELLISHMENTS

Embellishments are decorations that you add to the page to create a theme or enhance the layout. Some examples of embellishments are die-cuts, punch art, rubber stamps and stickers.

DIE-CUTS

Die-cut shapes and letters are cut out of varied weights of paper using a die-cutting machine. These machines and individual dies are expensive, so most people don't have their own. They are available to use at some paper supply and scrapbook stores for a fee to create just the die-cuts you want on your paper.

Purchase precut shapes in theme packages or make your own. Use cardstock, printed paper or even fabric and trace the shape you want using templates, coloring books or cookie cutters, or by printing clip art on the computer. Apply die-cuts to create headings, correspond to the theme or add focus. Plain paper die-cuts can be used to journal on when adding a story to your page.

PUNCH ART

Paper punches are considered mini die-cutting machines and create a variety of shapes and sizes. The "craft punch" is the most common type of punch available. It sits on a tabletop and has a button on the top. You slide a scrap of paper in the underside of the punch and press the button to create the shape. You can also get handheld punches in a variety of tiny shapes.

Punch shapes using acid-free paper, cardstock or adhesive-backed paper. With just a few punches, you can create an elegant design to enhance a theme on your page. Paper punches are also an economical way to use all those little scraps of paper that would be wasted. On the page below, leaves and layered butterflies complement the gentle, summer feeling.

Pictures are Timeless Treasures in our Family Heritage!

July 1966

Kirschner Family Reunions
Family, Food, Fun, Friends

We Remember Moments in our Lives

RUBBER STAMPS

Rubber stamping has been a fun and creative hobby that has grown leaps and bounds over the past decade. Rubber stamps offer a fast and easy way to embellish your album pages and come in an incredible variety of shapes, sizes and styles. There are different types of stamps, such as image stamps, mini stamps, alphabet stamps, frame stamps (which create borders around your photographs in a variety of shapes), photo corner stamps and journaling stamps (see chapter four for samples). They can add a touch of elegance to an album page and enhance the theme. Always use acid-free and fade-resistant dyes or pigment inks so the images will last as long as the pages themselves.

STICKERS

Strict archival conservators strongly suggest limiting the amount and number of chemicals that come into contact with photographs. We still don't know the environmental impact of long-term use of stickers. Make sure any stickers you use are made from acid-free, lignin-free paper, stable adhesives and nonreactive permanent inks. Do not put stickers directly on photographs. I suggest placing your photograph on a mat of buffered paper if the photo is going to be near a sticker. If there is any acid migration, it will migrate to the paper and not the photograph.

Rootstamps offer a whole line of genealogy and family history stamps available through mail order that are ideal for embellishing the pages of your album (and the correspondence you send requesting genealogy information).

Borderlines from Mrs. Grossman's, stickers designed specifically for borders, are ideal for heritage album pages.

CRAFTING YOUR OWN HERITAGE ALBUM

DISPLAYING MEMORABILIA

You can display just about anything in a heritage album. Some items might be too heavy or would be damaged if they were put in your album and handled a lot. You could take a color picture or make a color photocopy of the item to include on the album page. Many options are now available for displaying items such as coins, flowers, jewelry, ribbons, medals, event tickets, rocks and shells right in your album.

The 3D Keepers tiny treasure chests from DejaViews are ideal for displaying your three-dimensional items. They are acid-free and archival safe and come in a variety of geometric shapes, such as circles, squares, ovals and rectangles. Use an archival adhesive to seal and adhere these to your album page.

TREASURE WINDOWS

Safely display and preserve your memorabilia with acid-free pop-up windows for dimensional treasures. Treasure Windows come in packages with one pop-up window and two flat display windows, Mylar sheets for windows, border frames and die-cuts.

MEMORABILIA POCKETS

These are archival-safe, self-adhesive pockets in three different sizes for encapsulating items you want to display. They hold small, almost flat items such as coins, lockets of hair, sand from a beach vacation, ticket stubs and note cards. They have a full adhesive back that is ready to stick on your paper and a self-adhesive flap that you can close and open as often as you like. Memorabilia Pockets come in four varieties (three to four pockets per package): small, medium, large and assorted.

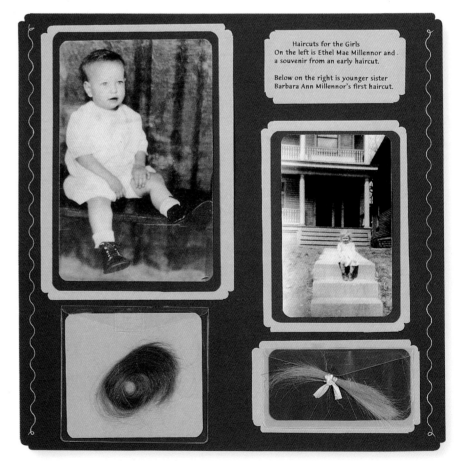

First haircuts are always a special moment in a child's life. I added baby pictures to these mementos of my two maternal aunts' first haircuts I found pressed between the pages of an old family book from my grandmother and their mother.

POCKET PAGES

Pocket pages are easy to create and offer a creative option for displaying miscellaneous items that you don't want to permanently adhere to a page. If an item has a front and a back side, it can be placed loose in the pocket and removed for easy viewing.

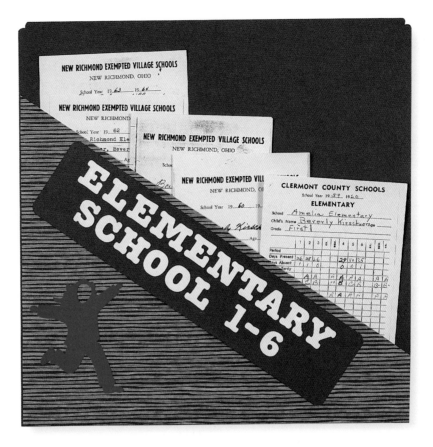

(above) Photocopies of my original elementary school report cards were made on similar acid-free paper and placed in this pocket page.

(left) The postcard pocket page was created using a lovely printed paper trimmed with decorative scissors. The pocket was glued to the cardstock on each side and on the bottom, leaving the top (or pocket) open. A second piece of the same decorative paper was trimmed and glued to the top of the page as a top border.

KEEPSAKE KEEPERS

Display three-dimensional items in these acid-free, archival-safe plastic trays. They come in two sizes, 8½"x11" and 12"x12". They include four to six different-shaped compartments totally enclosed and fully visible. They are hole-punched to fit into most scrapbooks.

Treasured Memories and Mementos

Grandma Anna Marie Millennor

October, 1956 Cincinnati, Ohio

Dave's Boutonnière from 1982

A gift from a friend in 1994

Grandma Marie's Necklace

Keep your memorabilia protected and totally visible in Keepsake Keepers. With two sizes (8½"x11" and 12"x12"), as well as being three-hole punched, they fit in most scrapbook albums.

GEMS
FROM
JOHN
GREENLEAF
WHITTIER

DEPARTED

Yes, dear departed, cher...
Could Memory's ha...
Your morning light, you...
From Time's gray ur...
Then might this restless heart...
This straining eye might clo...
And Hope her fainting pinions f...
While the fair phantoms rose...

But, like a child in ocean's arms,
We strive against the stream,
Each moment farther from the shore
Where life's young fountains glea...
Each moment fainter wave the fields,
And wider rolls the sea;
The mist grows dark,—the sun goes down
Day breaks,—and where are we?

CHAPTER 4
Journaling

Journaling is one of the most important elements in your heritage album. When others look through your album, they will read what you have written and it will bring the pictures and documents to life.

All families have stories to tell. Just ask. These stories are a way of connecting people with their pasts and should be recorded. Starting today, record information others tell you about family members. Interview the young members of the family, as well as the older members, to find out what is important to them. Find out their favorite games, what kinds of music they enjoy, what sports they play, who their best friends are, what pets they have, etc. Keep the information in a journal to reference when you put together album pages.

Journaling can be done by hand or with the aid of computers, stencils, die-cut letters, rubber stamps or alphabet stickers. Allow plenty of room for journaling; write about the story that goes with the pictures. If you don't know the story behind a picture right now, leave enough space to add information later. As family and friends look through your book, they may be able to tell you a story to include with the pictures.

WRITING: WHAT, HOW, WHERE?

When you begin to think about what to write, try to answer questions someone might have when looking at what's on the page.

- Who is this?
- Who are they related to?
- What were they doing?
- Where was the picture taken?
- When was it taken?
- Why do they look so happy or sad? (Include information about feelings, if known.)
- Whose car or house is in the picture?

Always include names, ages, dates, places and the event, if you know them.

Even if you don't have pictures to go with them, remember to include stories about family traditions and everyday events that, if not recorded, would be lost to future generations.

(left-hand page) My mother gave me a copy of her first driver's license. I documented the story of how she had learned to drive in a neighbor's field. I wanted to be sure the story wasn't lost over the years, as future generations would find it amusing how Grandma had learned to drive.

(right-hand page) I discovered this ambrotype photograph in the bottom of a shoebox from my grandmother. We didn't know who this man and woman were until I removed the picture and found an inscription, from March 1862. It turns out this is my great-great-grandmother. Her relationship to this man is still unconfirmed since she married another man around 1865.

JOURNALING TOOLS AND WRITING AIDS

There's an amazing variety of journaling tools available to help you create personal style on your pages. There are many rubber stamp designs that can be used. Using acid-free, archival-quality inks, you can either stamp directly on the album page with the stamped image and then journal, or stamp a piece of coordinating paper, add journaling, cut it out and adhere it to the album page.

If you don't have journaling "aids," a good method is to use a ruler and pencil to draw a light line where you are going to journal; if you use a separate piece of paper, cut the paper to the size you want and attach the paper to the album page.

Special books of classic material can help you find just the right phrase, scripture passage, poem, quotation or historical fact. Many poetry, historical and quotation books are available at the library, and specialty booklets are available at scrapbook supply stores. There are numerous Web sites that have hundreds of examples for journaling. Some of the most popular Web sites are referenced in the back of this book under Top Web Sites.

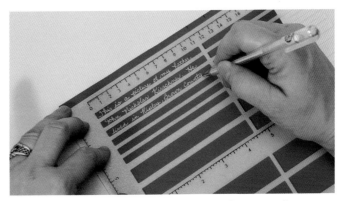

The Time Line from Tapestry in Time makes journaling directly on pages fast and easy. It's great for title pages and small, medium and large journaling.

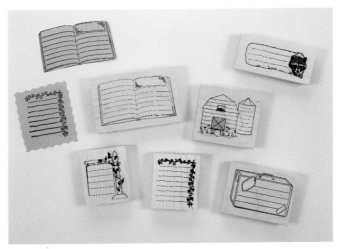

Scrapbookin' Stamps of Federal Way, Washington, has a line of rubber stamps created especially for scrapbook journaling. These stamps provide a quick and decorative way to add journaling lines for writing names, dates and memories that complement the theme of your album pages.

Chatterbox has created a line of books and journaling templates especially for scrapbook and heritage album makers. The books are filled with funny, touching and sentimental phrases to help you find just the right words to convey your message. EK Success Ltd. and Marvy Uchidal are just two companies that provide a wide variety of archival pens for journaling.

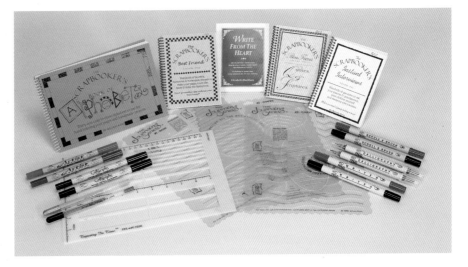

INTERVIEW QUESTIONS

Here are some sample questions to ask when interviewing family members to gather details about their lives that should be documented before the details are lost forever.

Childhood and Education

What were your favorite childhood games you played?

Who did you play with as a child?

What were your schools like?

Is your school still standing? Where is it located?

How far did you live from school and how did you get to school?

What subject in school was always the easiest for you?

What was your favorite subject in school and why?

What was your least favorite subject in school and why?

Who was your favorite teacher, and why was that person special?

Did you finish high school? Did you go to college?

Job

What was your first job?

What kinds of jobs have you had?

What did you want to be as an adult when you were a child?

How did you decide on your career?

Did you make enough money to live comfortably?

How long did you have to work each day at your job?

How old were you when you retired?

Marriage

How did you meet the person that you would later marry? Describe what your spouse was like at that time.

What was your first date like?

Did you know each other before you started dating? For how long?

How long did you go together before you got married?

When and where did you get married?

What kind of a wedding did you have? Who was there?

Did you have a honeymoon? Where did you go?

How would you describe your spouse?

How long have you been married?

Were you ever married to someone else? What happened to that relationship?

PAGES WITHOUT PICTURES

A primary reason for creating a heritage album is telling the story of your family history. Even if there are no pictures of family members to include in your album, you may have official documents and mementos that can expand on the basic information you have about birth and death dates. The journaling you include to tell the story of a person will help fill the gaps that would otherwise leave your heritage album incomplete.

Documenting and journaling details about the genealogical documents in your heritage album are essential. Remember to always include the source of the document in your journaling.

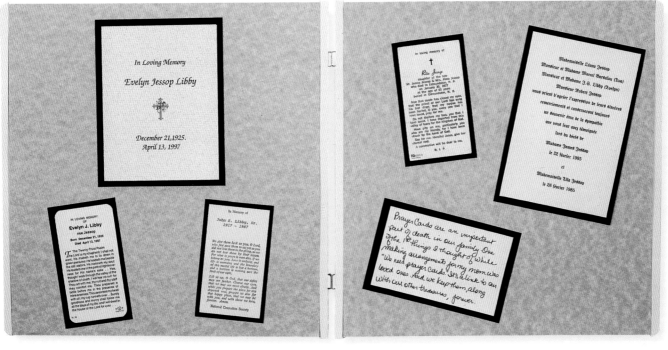

Even without pictures to go along with your documents, you can tell a great deal about an ancestor through journaling.

JOURNALING WHOLE PAGES

Don't be afraid to use a whole page in your album to write about family tradition; include special poems or scriptures, short biographies or a famous quote. Let your personality come through. Get other family members involved by asking them to write a story to go along with the pictures.

USE YOUR OWN HANDWRITING

Don't be intimidated by your own handwriting. It is perfectly acceptable. This is another feature that will become part of the heirloom to future generations.

You may want to practice your handwriting to keep the letters neat and consistent. If you are going to journal right on the page, you might want to practice on scrap paper. This way, you are sure it looks OK and that it will fit into the space for journaling.

Journaling in your own handwriting is one way to create prized pages. Just think how thrilled you would be if you had a history of your mother's early days in her own handwriting.

66

CRAFTING YOUR OWN HERITAGE ALBUM

JOURNALING THE HARD TIMES

It's easy to find good memories to journal in your album. It's more difficult to record those memories that caused sadness. Recording these memories, however, can play an important part in helping family members both deal with and heal from those difficult times in their lives. Some of the less joyful times that you can record through pictures and journaling include serious illness or injury, death, bankruptcy, legal conflicts and natural disasters, such as floods, fires, tornadoes and hurricanes. If you have pictures, add the story, including the highs and lows of the event. Tell the names of the family and friends involved, places, dates and the outcome of the event. It is important when presenting and preserving your family legacy that you record the entire history as accurately and fully as possible. Future generations should understand what their ancestors have gone through to fully appreciate their history.

The Flood of 1997 was devastating to thousands of families who lived along the Ohio River in Ohio, Kentucky and Indiana. These pictures show the results of one family member's hardship as a result of the fast-rising water and the mess that was left in the aftermath.

Computer journaling

Computer journaling takes a little more time, but it produces great results and is certainly very appropriate in a heritage album. Using the computer will allow you to type drafts of your stories, rewrite and polish them, and experiment with font and layout. The decision on whether to use a computer may depend on what's easiest for you.

Most printer inks are archival quality now, but you need to be sure before you begin your project. Call the printer manufacturers directly, and they will be able to tell you. Most home printers can only print on 8½"x11" pages right now. If you are using the larger 12"x12" pages, you will be printing on a separate piece of paper and then adding it to the album page.

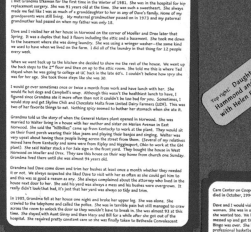

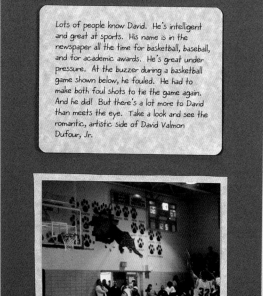

Computer journaling these pages made it fast and easy to include information that would be time-consuming to handwrite.

JOURNALING GENEALOGICAL FACTS

As part of your journaling, your album should include basic genealogical facts, such as names, birth and death dates, and relationships between family members ("parent of," "child of," etc.). Include as much information as you have on events in family members' lives, such as when and where they were born, when and where they were married, what they did for a living, what property they owned, and who their neighbors and friends were. These pieces of information will help family and friends piece together the family relationships. Remember, you are documenting your family history and this information is critical to the overall validity of your heritage album.

If you are including genealogy documents, include the "source" information. You must do your research and be sure the information you have is accurate and credible. If the document can be found as part of a court record, list the name of the court (indicate if it is local, state or federal court), city or town, volume, page number, document record number and date found, if known. If it is a church record, list the name and address of the church.

If you are including oral histories in your journaling, include the source of those also. In years to come, you may not remember the source of the information. If Aunt Maggie or Uncle Charles told you the story, include "Conversation with Aunt Maggie, 15 March 1999" or "Videotaped interview with Uncle Charles, 12 December 1998."

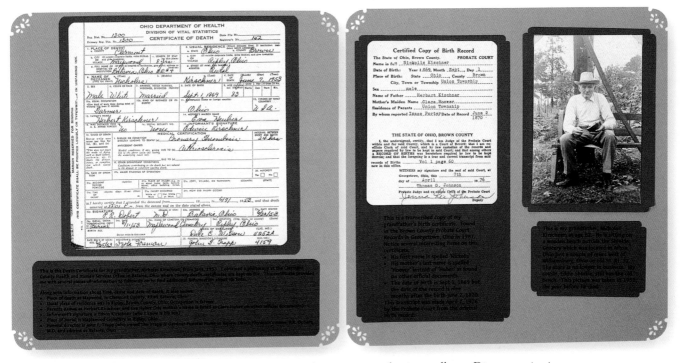

Copies of official genealogical documents are an essential asset to your heritage album. Discrepancies in information can be documented, as well as the source of the document.

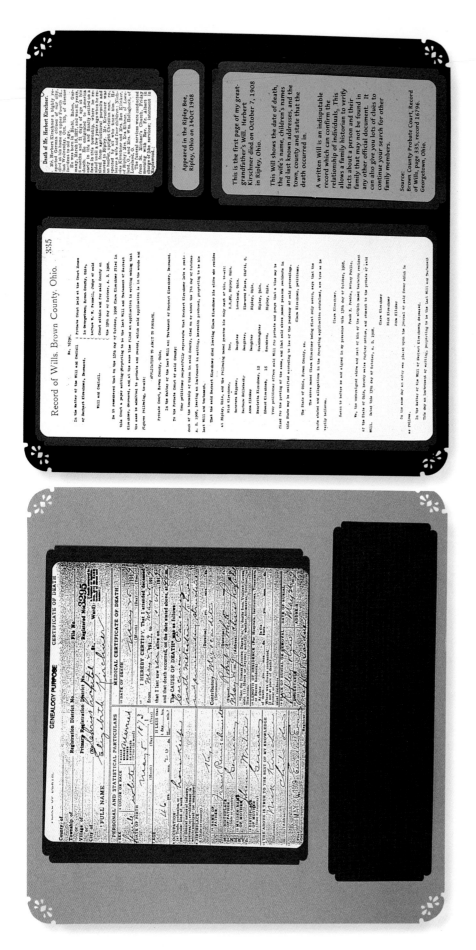

Including record details along with the source information on genealogy documents will show family members that the information has been verified and is accurate. It will also save you research time if you ever need to return to the original source to recheck information.

This is the first page of my great-grandfather's Will. Herbert Kirschner died on October 7, 1908 in Ripley, Ohio.

This Will shows the date of death, the wife's name, children's names and last known addresses, and the town, county and state that the death occurred in.

A written Will is an indisputable record which can confirm the relationship of individuals. This allows a family historian to verify facts about a person and their family that may not be found in any other official document. It can also give you lots of clues to continue your search for other family members.

Source:
Brown County Probate Court, Record of Wills, page 335, record 16796. Georgetown, Ohio.

A FINAL WORD ON JOURNALING

Which page will be more valuable to
future generations?

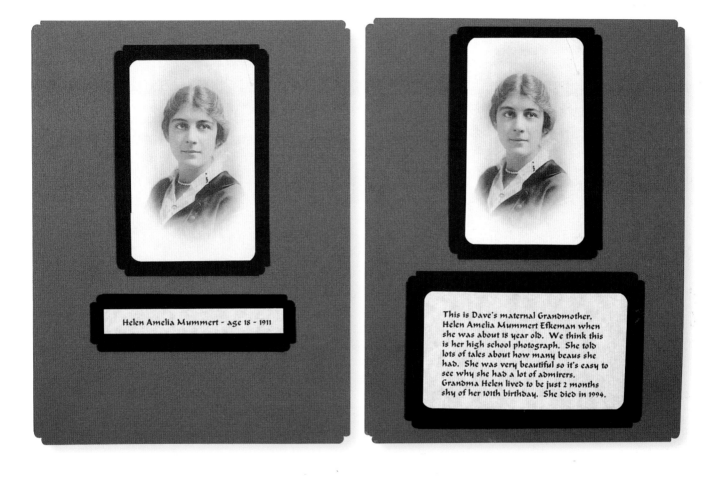

Helen Amelia Mummert - age 18 - 1911

This is Dave's maternal Grandmother,
Helen Amelia Mummert Efkeman when
she was about 18 year old. We think this
is her high school photograph. She told
lots of tales about how many beaus she
had. She was very beautiful so it's easy to
see why she had a lot of admirers.
Grandma Helen lived to be just 2 months
shy of her 101th birthday. She died in 1994.

CHAPTER 5
Genealogy Basics

One out of every seven people is actively working on some aspect of family history. Most people begin genealogy research out of curiosity about their family histories. They begin collecting names, dates and relationships, and then find themselves wanting to know more about the everyday lives of their ancestors.

Genealogy, by definition, is a recorded history of the descent of a person or family from an ancestor or ancestors. By researching and documenting your family history, you undergo the study of your ancestry. When most people reach their forties, they have a desire to preserve their family histories and share the family legacies with future generations. Once they have families of their own, they begin to realize how important it is to know details about family and ancestors.

The quest begins. Where did my ancestors come from? Who am I related to? Where did they live? You'll develop a stronger self-esteem and a deeper sense of belonging as your research progresses. You'll discover similar physical traits, persistent temperaments and consistent skills and talents that represent the intangible bonds that connect a family through generations.

YOUR FAMILY PUZZLE

The most common question any family historian or genealogist hears is, "How do I get started?" Most people start out researching their family trees (names, dates and relationships). At some point they become interested in researching more details of their predecessors' everyday lives. What were my ancestors like? Where did they live? What did they do for occupations? What were their hobbies? What did they do for entertainment and recreation? How far did they go in school? Were they rich, poor or somewhere in between? Are their houses or farms still standing?

Genealogy research is like a giant jigsaw puzzle. As you gather individual facts piece by piece, it may not seem like much. But then you'll discover a piece of information that connects several facts and your jigsaw puzzle begins to take shape. You need to decide what you want to research and just what questions you would like to have answered. If your response is "everything," it may take years to put all those pieces together or some may never be found. It really depends on how much information you are able to verify and how much time you have to spend researching. But every piece of the puzzle that you connect is so rewarding that it keeps you searching for the next clue year after year.

A Coluzzle Template was used to create this terrific layout. The Coluzzle Collage Template System allows you to create custom collage puzzles from your personal photographs with unique shapes such as a rectangle, star, heart, oval and bear.

GETTING STARTED

Basic genealogical research will have to be done in courthouses, libraries and archives. Most of the records you will investigate are not available on-line and may never be. You may need to sharpen your letter-writing skills if you are researching ancestors in an area of the country or a part of the world that you can't readily visit in person.

Unfortunately, the information you need may not always be available. Older relatives won't live forever and they hold the key to a lot of facts that you may not be able to discover without their help.

You may find another family member who is interested in working on the research with you. There are lots of benefits to working together. You will keep each other going as you share the information you uncover about your family history. If you live in different homes, you should each keep a copy of each other's information. That way, you won't have to start over to rebuild your documentation if a disaster strikes one of your homes.

Don't Judge Your Ancestors

One thing you should be prepared for as you start your pursuit of ancestors is that you may find out things you didn't think you'd find—some good and some not so good. Don't be too hasty to form an opinion of them. Be considerate and don't be judgmental. You don't know what their circumstances were. They had strengths and weaknesses, and sometimes they made mistakes. So if everyone you come across on your family tree isn't perfect, don't think of it as something bad. Just remember there are all kinds of trees with many kinds of leaves and not every leaf is perfect.

SUPPLIES

FILE FOLDERS

If you are just starting out, you can begin using color-coded file folders for different family members. Always list the last name first on the folder tab. You can then arrange the folders alphabetically by surname and then by first name. If your research is already underway, you can use color-coded labels on your current file folders. Try to keep up with your research by filing everything as soon as you acquire it.

FILING BOXES AND CABINETS

Depending on how much room you have for storing documents and how much you have to store, you'll need file boxes or a filing cabinet. Filing boxes are inexpensive and easily stack on top of each other. They can also be moved easily and be kept in a closet or under a table or desk. Filing cabinets may be available from office supply warehouses that offer large discounts on used filing cabinets.

THREE-RING BINDER AND NOTEBOOK

I recommend starting with a three-ring binder with loose-leaf notebook paper. The loose-leaf paper will allow you to rearrange your notes. You can add a few divider tabs as your research progresses and as you need more organized notes. You can also use a spiral notebook that opens on the side to keep all of your notes in, but it will be more difficult to keep related items together than with loose-leaf paper.

Use an archival pen with permanent ink rather than pencil whenever you can (some research libraries don't let you use pen while doing research, so check with them first if you are un-

Color coding your ancestor files is an easy way to keep track of all the information you will accumulate. Use a different color of folder for each family line to make retrieving family information easier.

A three-ring binder with loose-leaf paper, a small notebook, some index cards and an archival pen will help make the information you collect at the library or at family gatherings easy to keep track of and to research in detail later.

sure). If your notes get wet, permanent ink won't run or fade. Pencil will smudge after a while and you may have illegible notes. If I know I will be around family members, I carry a small notebook and pen to write notes; you never know when someone will tell you something that will be a big clue in your research.

USING FORMS TO BEGIN

Start with yourself and work backwards to create a basic family tree. The two best aids you can begin with in your genealogical research are the ancestral or pedigree chart and family group sheets. An ancestral chart is for recording an individual's direct-line ancestry. It usually includes that person's parents, grandparents, great-grandparents and so on, but does not include brothers, sisters, aunts, uncles and other relatives. There is a sample ancestral chart in the forms section in the back of this book for you to make copies of and use in your research.

A family group sheet is a form that presents genealogical information about a family—a husband, a wife and their children. A family group sheet usually includes birth, death and marriage dates and the place each of those occurred. There is a sample family group sheet in the forms section.

Begin by filling in as much of the information on these forms as you can; you may be surprised at just how much information you already know about your family and ancestors. Once you have as much information as you know on the sheets, it is time to begin gathering your genealogical research from other souces.

The ancestral chart and family history forms are a great way of getting started. They will help you determine what information you have and what you are missing so you can begin interviewing family members for the missing details. These forms came from *Unpuzzling Your Past Workbook* by Emily Croom (Better way Books).

Family Group Sheet of the __John KRAMER__ Family

John Frederick KRAMER (Full name of husband)	Birth date 30 Jan 1899
Robert John KRAMER (His father)	Birth place Kent, S.C.
Cynthia Woods (His mother with maiden name)	Death date 14 Dec 1978
	Death place Beaumont, TX
	Burial place Maple Grove Cemetery Beaumont, TX
Rebecca Anne BROWN (Full maiden name of wife)	Birth date 7 May 1901
Charles T. Brown (Her father)	Birth place Beaufort, NC
Caroline Cannon (Her mother with maiden name)	Death date 3 Apr 1983
	Death place Beaumont, TX
	Burial place Maple Grove Cemetery Beaumont, TX
Other Spouses	Marriage date, place, etc. 16 Nov 1921 Beaufort, NC

Children of this marriage	Birth date & place	Death date, place, & burial place	Marriage date, place & spouse
John Frederick KRAMER	11 Nov 1922 Beaufort, NC	15 Nov 1922 Beaufort, NC	
Elizabeth Anne KRAMER	10 Oct 1924 Beaufort, NC	15 Jul 1998 Beaufort, NC	Robert J. Williams 17 Aug 1945 Charleston, SC
Frank L KRAMER	15 Jul 1926 Beaufort, NC	3 Apr 1988 Rome, GA	Charlotte Meyer 12 Nov 1949 Savannah, GA

Five-Generation Chart # 1- KRAMER
using ahnentafel numbers
Lineage of KRAMER-BROWN
who is #1 on chart #
b = birth date & place
m = marriage date & place
d = death date & place

#2 John Kramer
b 30 Jan 1899
m 16 Nov 1924
d 14 Dec 1978

#1 Elizabeth Anne
b 10 Oct. 1924
Beaufort, NC
m
d 15 Jul 1998
Spouse Robert J Williams

#3 Rebecca Anne Brown
b 7 May 1901
Beaufort, NC
d 3 Apr 1983
Beaumont, TX

4 Robert John KRAMER
b 2 Feb 1867 Boston, MA
m 9 Apr 1893
d 12 Sept 1951 Kent, SC

5 Cynthia Woods
b 18 Jun 1868 Carter Cove, SC
d 20 May 1957 Kent, SC

6 Charles T Brown
b 3 Sept 1879 Brownsville, NC
m 6 May 1899
d 29 Oct 1958 Beaufort, NC

7 Caroline Cannon
b 4 Feb 1880 Beaufort, NC
d 23 Jul 1953 Beaufort, NC

8 Samuel J Kramer
b 04 Oct 1841
m
d abt. 1932

9 Elizabeth Johnson
b 11 Sept 1843
d unknown

10 Joshua Woods
b abt 1840
m
d

11 Anna Fraymer
b 16 Oct 1844
d 24 Jan 1908

12 Francis Brown
b 22 Sept 1839
m
d abt. 1917

13 Magdalene Swisher
b 15 Jul 1841

14 Charles Cannon
b abt 1840
m
d

15 Grace Beaker
b abt 1848
d unknown

16
17
18
19
20 Frederick Woods
21 Annabelle ?
22
23
24
25
26 Jacob Swisher
27 Clara ?
28
29
30
31

See Chart

Compiled by:

INTERVIEW RELATIVES AND TAKE NOTES

Gathering information from relatives can be very helpful. Always take notes when you are talking to family or friends about family history. Once your family and friends begin talking about old times, they will tell you many interesting stories. You might not catch some of the important details if you try to take notes and listen at the same time. Always check with people first, but use a tape recorder if they feel comfortable with being recorded as they talk. That way you can catch all of the stories and have plenty of time to write or type your notes from the tapes at a later time. Always record the date and event or person you were talking to on the tape itself so you will remember when and where the conversations took place.

Relatives can give you information about your family and ancestors that can save you hundreds of hours of initial research. They can give you information about where family members lived, where they worked, what churches they attended and what cemeteries they are buried in. These are all great clues to get you started on checking the facts. The memories of relatives, especially older relatives, are not as reliable as you may think. Be careful never to accept this information as fact until you have checked the information through official sources.

PLACES TO SEARCH

After you complete your basic family tree chart, you probably have quite a bit more information about your family history than you thought. You will also need to find and fill in the missing information to make the documentation complete.

Here are some suggestions on other resources to look at to locate some of that missing information.

adoption papers
announcements
awards/plaques
baptism papers
bonds
bookplates
canceled checks
christening records
citations
citizenship papers
confirmations
death certificates
deeds
diaries
diplomas
disability papers
discharge papers

divorce papers
employment records
engagement
  announcements
engraved jewelry
estate records
family Bibles
family histories
firearm registrations
friendship quilts
funeral books
greeting cards/lists
hospital records
journals
jury summons
land grants
leases

letters
library cards
loan papers
medical records
membership records
memorial cards
motor vehicle
  registrations
needlework samplers
newspapers
obituaries
passports
photographs
school records
scrapbooks

EARLY PHOTOGRAPHS

Let's look at early photographs and see what kind of information we can learn from them. Before modern color film was invented, there were several processes for developing and printing pictures. Being able to identify which kind of picture you have may help you identify an ancestor by the date or time period the photograph was taken. Some older types of photographs may also need special considerations for storage, rather than putting them in a protective sleeve in an album.

There are several good books available at your local bookstore and library that will help you learn more about photographs and documents and how to care for them. One of the better books to help you identify early photographs is by Craig A. Tuttle, *An Ounce of Preservation: A Guide to the Care of Papers and Photographs.*

CALOTYPE OR TALBOTYPE

The first real photographs were calotype or talbotype. This process was used from 1835 to the mid-1850s. Silver iodide was applied to a sheet of paper that was put in the camera. It was developed in gallic acid, making a negative image. A positive print was then made. The images were grainy and dull, especially compared to the daguerreotype process. Calotype and talbotype images are usually badly faded, due to incomplete developing methods. Since these were printed on paper, you would store them as you would other photographs, in photo sleeves or acid-free photo boxes.

DAGUERREOTYPE

The daguerreotype process was used from 1839 to the mid-1850s. It was

the first commercially successful photographic process. A positive image was produced on a copper plate that had been coated with silver and exposed to iodine vapors to make it light sensitive. The plate was put into the camera, exposed, then heated over mercury. It made a sharp detailed image, but daguerreotypes are very fragile. Usually, they were put into wooden cases (which were padded with silk or velvet) to protect them. These images cost about $5, which was expensive during that time. If any restoration work needs to be done to these types of photographs, it should be done by a professional.

COLLODION/WET PLATE PROCESS

Collodion was a solution of guncotton fibers, potassium iodide, silver nitrate, alcohol and ether. The exposure and development of the collodion negatives had to be done while the plate was wet, therefore the name "wet plate." This process made great detail and contrast in the picture. There were two types of pictures using this process: ambrotypes and tintypes.

AMBROTYPES

The ambrotype process was used from 1854 to the 1870s. The collodion solution was coated on polished glass. When exposed, it made a negative image that was then backed with black paper or cloth to give a positive. Ambrotypes are similar to daguerreotypes, since they were also put into protective cases. However, an ambrotype's surface is not mirror like and these photographs were much more fragile than daguerreotypes and took longer to expose. Ambrotypes were

cheaper to produce though, making them very popular.

TINTYPES

Tintypes were used from 1856 to the 1890s. These images were created by layering the collodion solution onto sheets of lacquered metal. This produced a direct positive image. These images were very inexpensive, from 10 to 25 cents, and were used for portrait photography. They were popular due to their durability, price and speed of development. The cases were replaced with paper folders, and any tinting of the photograph was protected with varnish. Tintypes were extremely popular during the Civil War, when almost every soldier could afford to have his picture in uniform sent home to his family. There is actually no tin in tintypes. The base is thin black iron and a small magnet will be attracted to it.

ALBUMEN PRINTS

Albumen prints were used between 1847 and the mid-1890s and produced very detailed images. Glass plate negatives were coated with a mixture of egg whites, silver nitrate and sodium chloride. The process was limited to landscape photography in the earliest years because a very long exposure was required. In 1850 the introduction of albumen-sensitized paper led to high resolution portraits. The prints were mounted onto cards because the thin paper was prone to tear or curl. The cards that the photos are mounted on can help date the photographs. Look for other clues listed on the facing page.

These ambrotype photographs are from 1862. The woman is my great-great-grand-mother and an unknown close friend of hers. The tintype is from around the 1870s but the person has not been identified yet. These were discovered in an old box of photographs of my grandmother's.

Other Photo Clues

There are other clues to look at when researching your photographs. Look at the clothes your ancestors wore. There was a big change in the look of clothes, especially men's clothes, around 1900. Clothes were readily available in stores and took on a significantly different look. There are books in the library that will help you identify different time periods based on fashion and clothing. If are having trouble pinpointing the time period of some old pictures, this might be a good way to narrow it down to a specific 10-to 20-year period.

Look at other things in the background, such as the houses, automobiles, toys, landmarks and street signs. These are all valuable clues to help you get one step closer to your ancestors.

These postcard photographs were taken between 1880 and 1905 and are in re-markable condition.

DOCUMENTING YOUR SOURCES

From the start of your research, always keep an accurate, complete record of the source material you use. You may need to look up additional information and won't want to waste time trying to figure out where you got the information you have. You also don't want to waste time duplicating research you've already done.

It is a good idea to document your information sources on your album pages. This will allow your family and future generations to verify that the information is correct. If you do not cite your sources, it will be difficult for anyone reading the family's history to know if the information in your family tree is accurate.

Source Documentation

• If you got the information from a book, microfilm record or any other document, record where you found that item. Be sure to cite the library, county archive, or building that you found the information in along with the call number.

• If the information is from a book, list the author, the title of the source, where it was published, where it is located, the year it was written, the call number, the page number, the document number, the reference number or any other identifying number.

• If the information is from your personal knowledge, make sure you note that when you cite your sources.

• If the information is provided by another family member or genealogist, whether professional or amateur, provide the person's name, address and telephone number along with the date the information was given to you. (Don't include personal information about other people if you publish information on the Internet or other public source.)

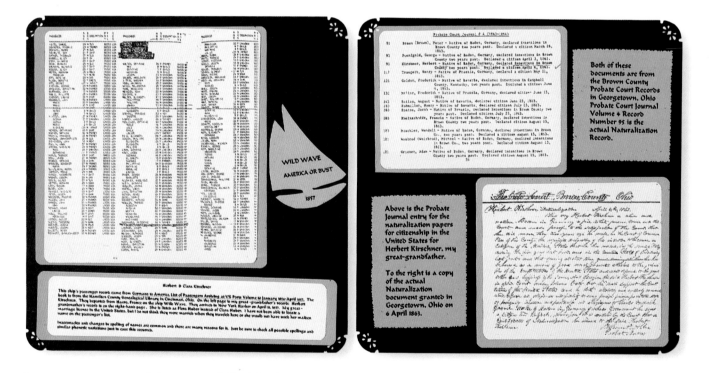

It is important to record the source of all of the documents and information you uncover during your research of family history. This eliminates researching the same files more than once. It also helps speed up your research if you do need to go back to the same record for an additional piece of information.

RESEARCH LOG

Keeping a detailed research log saves me a lot of time. There are times when I am unable to do research for several months. When I resume my investigation, I check my research log and pick up right where I left off. Keep track of all records you search even if you don't find anything. Write the name of the research building or facility, the town or city name, date, what information you found and the page number of the book or record. Make notes about what you were searching for and whether you found anything. This will save you hours of otherwise wasted time by not searching the same records more than once. There are sample research logs available in the forms section that you can copy and use for the library and courthouse.

If you get stuck in your research and don't seem to be making much progress, reread your research logs. Something might jump out at you that you overlooked before. Every once in a while, go back and look through the documents you accumulate on each family member. You might find something you either overlooked or that just makes more sense with new information you discovered on that person.

Library Research Log

Ancestor's Name: KRAMER

Objective(s): Military Records   Locality: Charleston, SC

DATE	LOCATION/CALL NUMBER	SOURCE DESCRIPTION (Title, Author, Year, Record #, ISBN #)	COMMENTS (Results of Search, Follow-up Required, Names Researched)	Document Number
6/6/99	B 716.23	Civil War Index #4	No KRAMERS	—
6/6/99	T439.19A	C.W. Index #12	Johnson, James	Vol. 4 pg 16
6/6/99	Microfilm #291	Copy of Soldiers List	Johnson, James	#553
6/6/99	Index	Charleston Times	No KRAMERS	June 1860 – Dec 1861

Prepared by:

Date:

Courthouse Research Log

Ancestor's Name: KRAMER

Objective(s): Military Land Grant   Courthouse Name & Location: Charleston SC

Assorted Courthouse Records

			Military Land Grant Records from Civil War
Adoptions	(Grants)	Marriage Records	Supoena
Appeals	Tax Lists	Name Changes	Voter Registration
Autopsy	Divorce Petitions	Naturalization Petition	Wills
Bankruptcy	Estate Appraisals	Naturalization Decree	Warrants
Birth Certificates	Guardians	Notice of Sales	
Birth Records	Jury Duty	Notice to Creditors	Other
Certificate of Freedom	Liens	Notice to Heirs	
Civil Suits	Marriage Applications	Orphan Records	
Death Certificates	Marriage License	Petition to Freedom	
Deeds	Marriage Certificate	Real Estate	

Findings

Date Researched	Volume Number	Record No. & Page No.	Results of Research
6-6-99	38		NO KRAMERS
6-6-99	48-53-58		NO KRAMERS
6-6-99	63	14 pg. 168	Samuel John Kramer Copy of document made
6-6-99	74	28 pg 315	FRANK BROWN copy made of document

Prepared by:

Date:

You must have an established research plan before you begin your quest for information, whether it is on-site at a library or courthouse or on-line using the Internet.

PRIMARY AND COMPILED SOURCES

There are two basic types of sources you can obtain genealogy information from: primary and compiled. Primary sources are original, factual records, such as birth and death certificates, marriage records, wills and land deeds, or photocopies of original documents or authentic government records.

Compiled sources (sometimes called secondary sources) are records that have been copied or transcribed and are subject to errors such as oral histories from family members and published family histories. These may contain mistakes, so don't be tempted to use them without going to the original records. Compiled sources should be considered in your research and sometimes prove to be useful. They often provide clues that may lead you to factual primary sources at a later time.

Finding official copies of primary documents to validate your research is the ultimate goal of genealogical research.

On page three of a letter from my great-aunt to my grandmother, I discovered the information I needed to confirm her wedding date. This letter was used as a secondary source document that led me to obtaining a copy of the original marriage license, which is the primary source.

LOCAL RECORDS

There are a lot of official records kept at the local town hall or county courthouse. Birth certificates, marriage records, death certificates and probate records, such as wills, petitions, estate tax records and guardianship documents, are just a few. If you are unable to visit these places in person, you might request records by mail. It is a good idea to telephone the office to find out if someone can do the research for you and what the cost is. When making a request by mail, include the full name, dates and specific information about the document you are requesting. Also include a stamped, self-addressed envelope.

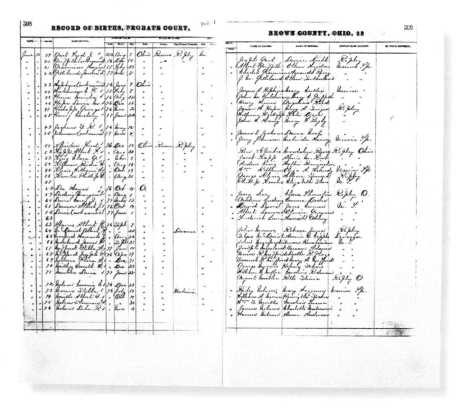

Copies of divorce papers and estate wills are just two examples of primary documents found in local probate court records.

Historical primary records in courthouses come in a variety of styles and contain various information. Each county of a state may have used different documents to record the same information. If you can obtain a photocopy of the document for your files, it is best to get one. You may need to look over this document many times in the future.

CRAFTING YOUR OWN HERITAGE ALBUM

STATE RECORDS

Most state archive offices keep duplicate copies of vital records (birth, death and marriage) at the state level. Each state has its own guidelines and fees for researching and obtaining documents. You'll need to check with each office to find out what information you need to supply when requesting information for genealogical research. Information on specific state offices and addresses is available through the public library and on the Internet. Some states will also forward your request to the local office if they do not have duplicate copies at the state level. Check university archives also. They usually have a published guide to their holdings, which can be extremely helpful if your research is concentrated in one particular state.

Information You May Find at State Level

- state land records

- tax rolls from county or from state assessments

- state pension records

- colonial, territorial or state census records

- vital statistics registry, which is primarily birth and death records

- Native American records, especially in Oklahoma

- vehicle registrations and drivers' licenses

- voter registrations and poll tax records

Birth and death records are usually available at the Bureau of Vital Statistics or the Department of Public Health. These may also be available at the county level.

FEDERAL RECORDS

The National Archives and Records Administration (NARA) in Washington, DC, contains a wealth of information about individuals whose names appear in census records, military records and pension files, ship and passenger lists, land records and many other types of documents of interest to both beginning and experienced genealogists. Private researchers can use both original and microfilmed records. There are research rooms, microfilm reading equipment and document copying facilities available at all locations. If you are unable to visit the archive offices in person, you can obtain documents through the mail.

The National Archives conducts comprehensive genealogical workshops each year. Some of the topics covered in these programs include an introduction to genealogy and researching primary records, such as census schedules, military service records, passenger lists, and ethnic genealogy research. The fee for classes is nominal. They offer research guides, genealogy books, pamphlets, indexes to microfilm records, and other information for sale.

There are regional branches of the National Archives scattered throughout the country, which house regional records and microfilm copies of some records stored at NARA in Washington, DC.

The National Archives has custody of millions of records relating to persons who have had dealings with the federal government—a great resource for genealogists at all levels.

CHURCH RECORDS

Church records usually contain information about marriages, baptisms and burials. These records may also contain information about godparents, witnesses at marriages and members who moved on to different congregations, which can lead to other family names and documents for you to research.

Church records can be difficult to locate. These are considered private records, not public, so you won't find them in the courthouses. In older churches, the minister usually kept the records. They were usually passed on to the next pastor but were sometimes stored for safekeeping and became lost or forgotten. If you can locate the church your ancestors attended, begin by writing a letter to the current minister. If the records can be located, the minister is usually willing to search them and give you as much information as they have about the person you are seeking information on.

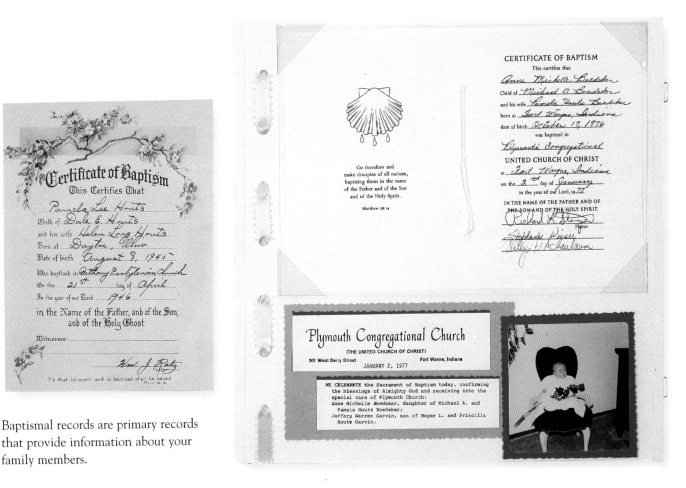

Baptismal records are primary records that provide information about your family members.

OTHER SOURCES

GENEALOGICAL AND HISTORICAL SOCIETIES

Genealogical and historical societies usually have offices on county and state levels and can be a great source of assistance to you. They can offer advice and help on where to locate specific records for ancestors you are researching. Some county offices have area specific information that has been donated specifically for genealogy and historical researchers. Many of these groups have special ties and volunteers who work at the local public libraries with genealogical holdings.

Join a local genealogy society if you don't belong to one. Share your interest and passion for family history research. This group of people will share your enthusiasm and help you get over hurdles you might encounter. Members usually have all levels of expertise and experience in researching and can help you get started. Most societies publish a periodical for that locale that can be helpful to you. If you are doing long-distance research, also join the society in the area your research will be concentrating in. Someone there may steer you in the right direction and help you find information that you can't find on your own.

PUBLIC LIBRARIES

The resources available at local public libraries vary in scope. You'll have to review the card catalog to find out what research material is available at libraries in your area. Most public libraries with an interest in genealogy have some of these records available for you: military record indexes, printed family histories, some local histories, census indexes, passenger list indexes, local newspaper on micro-

film, local cemetery listings, books on the basics of genealogy, old city directories, Internet access and information on local genealogy and historical societies.

Some local libraries have handwritten letters and family histories in vertical file folders that have not yet been made part of the permanent collections. Be sure to check these files. They are a great source of firsthand information on local families and history in that area. Many of our ancestors migrated and settled to different parts of the United States and Canada. You might find information on some of your ancestors in an area you didn't know they were in.

FAMILY HISTORY LIBRARY OF SALT LAKE CITY

Established in 1894 under the auspices of The Church of Jesus Christ of Latter-day Saints, the Family History Library contains the largest collection of genealogical records in the world. It has over two million rolls of microfilm containing copies of original records from more than one hundred countries. The records include church, land, probate, vital, census and other records of genealogical importance. The records at the library are found in many media including books, microfilm, microfiche and computer databases.

There are over three thousand local Family History Centers throughout the world where you can search computer records and indexes on-line, request copies of microfilm to search and obtain copies of original records for your research. The centers are usually part of the church and staffed by volunteers. They may operate as a

major research center, be a very small attachment to the local church or be any variation in between. The local centers have a core collection of genealogical information relating to the areas in which they are located. Most of them will also have access to microfilm and fiche through a rental program with the Family History Library in Salt Lake City.

In spring 1999, the church launched the Family Search Internet Genealogy Service. The new site is designed to help people find and share family history information. It gives you access to extensive genealogical resources gathered by the Church of Jesus Christ of Latter-day Saints. It is available on the WWW at: www.familysearch.org.

If you would like more information, the Web site for The Church of Jesus Christ of Latter-day Saints is www.lds.org. The library is located at 35 North West Temple Street, Salt Lake City, Utah 84150, (801) 240-2331.

CEMETERIES

Local cemeteries may provide a lot of information about your ancestors. Sometimes whole families are buried together, so some of your puzzle pieces may come together. Most local libraries and genealogical society offices have indexes of local cemeteries that can help identify which cemeteries you may want to visit. Many of the rural cemeteries have never been documented, so you may have problems finding information.

Cemetery names have changed over the years. A cemetery may become known by the family who has the most members buried there. You may find two cemeteries in one township called "Old Tate Cemetery" and "New Tate Cemetery." Your death certificate may just say Tate Cemetery, which means you'll need to do research in both to find the right one. If the cemetery is associated with a church, the church may have records,

or they may be kept at the town hall or municipal building.

Always take a notebook and a camera to the cemetery with you. Take pictures of the headstones and document where the grave sites are situated. You may find headstones with family names on them that you were not aware of. Record these names and dates on film and in your notebook for follow-up research.

Maplewood Cemetery is on U.S. 52 in Ripley, Brown County, Ohio. The top headstones are Bev's grandparents. The headstone at the bottom left is for Bev's great-grandparents. The marker below is the section where most of the Kirschner family members are buried. Herbert and Clara Kirschner are not buried in this section. They are buried with their son Frank and his wife Victoria Kirschner.

Taking a camera on cemetery visits is an easy way to record headstones you find that have family surnames on them. You can then do research on the names at a later time to see if they are in fact your family members' names.

NEWSPAPERS

Newspapers contain information especially helpful in genealogy research. They do contain information about courthouse records, such as news accounts of trials, land transfers, estate settlement notices, lawsuits and other legal announcements. Most newspapers are not considered public record and cannot be found with courthouse records. The best place to find newspapers is in local and state archives and in libraries. Most local libraries have microfilm or microfiche of old newspapers available to the public for that town and surrounding counties.

Since newsprint deteriorates very rapidly, photocopy clippings you want to preserve. Be sure to record the source information so you will know exactly where and when the information appeared.

MARRIAGES

Nineteenth-century newspapers usually printed news concerning nuptial agreements. Marriages appeared under that caption or within columns of local news.

BIRTHS

Birth notices were not commonly reported in nineteenth-century newspapers. During the early 1900s, the printing of birth announcements in local papers gradually became a popular custom.

OBITUARIES

An obituary may provide a biographical sketch, giving factual information and some insight into the personality of the deceased. Few nineteenth-century newspapers, however, published more than brief notices of death, un-

less the deceased was a prominent citizen or the family paid to have the news published.

OTHER ITEMS

Legal notices concerning estates may indicate death dates and heirs. Court dockets and lists of taxpayers, subscribers, county fair prize winners, and so on can be helpful in establishing the residence of persons at particular times.

It is often fun and rewarding to search several years of local news about the community where your family lived. You can discover facts that can be presumed ("Mr. and Mrs. Charles Banks took Sunday dinner with their daughter Mrs. Steven Levy" indicates that Mrs. Levy's maiden name was Banks), as well as details about the local community.

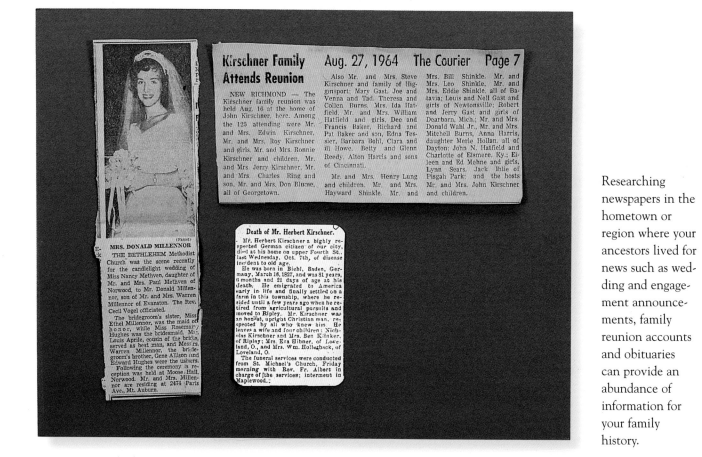

Researching newspapers in the hometown or region where your ancestors lived for news such as wedding and engagement announcements, family reunion accounts and obituaries can provide an abundance of information for your family history.

USING TECHNOLOGY

GENEALOGY COMPUTER SOFTWARE

Using genealogy software can make it very simple to store names, dates and unlimited facts about your history. Along with information about each person's personality, education and medical history, you can use a scanner and add documents and photographs. Most software allows you to print customized genealogy reports and forms with your family history information.

Once you begin accumulating lots of names, genealogy management software will allow you to access information quickly and easily. Instead of putting all of my family lines in one big file, I set up different family files for each of my family lines (one for my father's and one for my mother's), as well as for my husband's family. It is much easier to keep your family records organized this way. Otherwise, the files may become so big that it is difficult to print reports and family history information on one branch of the family line.

There are many commercial genealogy programs available. The best advice I have is to do your research. I've found that you usually get what you pay for, which means if you pay only a few dollars for something, you won't get many features. Most really good programs run between $40 and $80. Talk to other genealogists you meet to find out what software they use and why. This may help you figure out what is best for you before you buy the wrong product.

Be sure that the software program you choose is GEDCOM capable. GEDCOM is a standard file format used for exchanging data between different genealogy databases and programs.

I use a couple of different genealogy software packages. Each one does things a little differently. I use Family Tree Maker software from Broderbund for my family history files. Family Tree Maker also has one of the largest and most useful genealogy Web sites on the Internet. It offers over one hundred CD-ROMs that can help you speed up your research. It can also help you prepare for a library visit or obtain a documented copy of information from a state or federal office.

THE INTERNET AND WORLD WIDE WEB

Basic hardware you'll need to access the Internet is a personal computer, a modem and a telephone line. You don't have to have a separate telephone line to access the Internet, but you may not be able to use your telephone while you are on-line, depending on the service provider you select.

There are many Internet service providers available. America Online (AOL), Prodigy and CompuServe are three of the most popular. Other providers include AT&T, MCI and local telephone companies. Information on all of these providers and many more is available in personal computer magazines at local bookstores and libraries. The providers don't all offer the same services or the same pricing. Do your research and select the one that best fits your needs.

The Internet will allow you to talk (using electronic mail, or E-mail) with people anywhere in the world as if they were next door. You can contact other genealogists in countries such as Canada, Europe, Great Britain, Africa and Australia much easier than ever before. There are specific guidelines for using E-mail and dos and don'ts that you need to learn before you start sending messages. Otherwise, you can easily offend someone on the receiving end of the message.

Before sending detailed, lengthy E-mail messages to people you have not corresponded with before, send short introductory messages telling them about your interest in genealogy. Find out if they share your interest in family history before you send them details on your request. Remember, they may have to pay for each E-mail message they send and receive, so don't waste their time or money without knowing they want to hear from you. Otherwise, you may cost yourself friends and potential research partners.

The Internet will help you with your genealogy research. The vast holdings of the Family History Library in Salt Lake City are just being introduced on a new Web site (see Top Genealogy Web Sites, page 122). But you won't be able to do all of your research there. You will still have to visit libraries, courthouses and genealogy society offices, and write letters to places you can't visit in person.

Regardless of whether you are searching in person or on-line, start with an established search plan. The research log included in the forms section will give you a form to help keep track of what you have researched. Decide what you want to look for, and keep track of where you have been and what you have looked at.

If you are new to using the Internet and searching on-line, I recommend that you look at some of the books listed in the resource guide. Go to the library or local bookstore and flip through some of these books to learn more about "going on-line."

SEARCHING ETHNIC AND SPECIALTY RESOURCES

There are vast resources available for specialty researching. I've included just a few of the sources that are geared specifically toward ethnic and specialty research to start with. As you use the library and the Internet more, your list of resources will grow quickly.

There is a list of the Top Genealogy Web Sites on page 122; start with them, and before long you will be on your way. Remember to keep track of any good sites you come across so you can use them again.

AFRICAN-AMERICAN ANCESTRY

Many African-Americans who believe they are descendants of slaves erroneously assume that there are no records relating to their ancestors' lives. If you are searching post-1864, you would use the same sources as for any other group, such as census records, vital records and oral family histories. Some former slaves, but not all of them, took the names of their owners when they were emancipated. For pre-1864 records, check plantation books and slave advertisements. Since slaves were considered property, records might also be found in deed books and in probate records of their owners. There are numerous African-American newspapers that can be researched, as well as a couple of books that can help you locate the newspaper that you may be looking for. Try *A Reference Guide to Afro-American Publications and Editors, 1827–1946*, by Vilma Raskin Potter, Iowa State University Press. A second book is *The Afro-American Press and Its Editors*, Irvine Garland Penn, 1969.

Other places to contact for information:

Afro-American Historical and Genealogical Society, Inc.
P.O. Box 73086
Washington, DC 20056-3086
Telephone: (202) 234-5330

http://www.msstate.edu/Archives/History/afrigen/
This is a must-see site for African ancestry research. There is an on-line newsletter, a list of frequently asked questions (FAQs), and links to many other Web sites of interest to those researching African-American ancestry.

http://www.nara.gov/publications/microfilm/blackstudies/blackstd.html
The National Archives and Records Administration (NARA) provides an on-line list of the select catalog of NARA microfilm publications, which identifies records and other resources that are available from NARA pertaining to African-Americans.

NATIVE AMERICANS

Tracing your Native American ancestral line can be a real challenge since there are few written records prior to the mid-19th century. Native Americans' ancestors fall into two basic categories: those who remained in organized tribes or bands and those who blended into non-Native American society.

There are two types of tribal records that exist. Records of tribes that were made wards of the state and lived on reservations are the first. The second are records for tribes of the Five Civilized Tribes (Cherokee, Choctaw, Chickasaw, Creek and Seminole) which were primarily from the southeastern part of the United States and relocated in Oklahoma.

Most of the Five Civilized Tribes' records can be found in the Oklahoma Historical Society, in the National Archives Regional Office in Fort Worth, Texas, and at the University of Oklahoma's Western History Collection.

Some nontribal Federal census records are available through the National Archives and its regional branches, as well as many of the historical societies in states where reservations are located. There are many books available from research libraries and National Archives that can help you locate records and research your Indian ancestry.

http://www.indians.org./tribes/
The American Indian Tribal Directory lists all of the tribes that are officially recognized by the United States government. The directory list can be searched by tribe, city, state or city and state. Also, look in the National Archives at http://www.nara.gov/publications/microfilm/amerindians/indians.html.

ADOPTEES

Although the search for your biological parents may be difficult if you are adopted, it is not impossible. There are many resources available to help you in your search. The best place to start is the library; check to see what books are available to help you get started in your search.

http://www.cyndislist.com/adoption.htm
This Web site will link you to several sites geared specifically to adoption-related research topics.

IN CONCLUSION

I hope this book has provided you with the inspiration to begin (or continue) documenting your family history and creating your heritage album. I believe that you will find out more about yourself as you search for your ancestors. You'll discover your creative side as you lay out your pages and tell the story of your ancestors. You'll discover that you might enjoy being a private detective searching through old record books and taking notes every time someone mentions "the good old days." You'll discover new friends in library and genealogy offices wherever you go who share your passion for knowing the little things about your family—such as what clothes they wore, where they worked and what good and bad things happened to them. These are some of the things that make you who you are. Happy hunting—and show off those album pages to everyone who is interested. You might just inspire others to start searching their family heritages!

When using printed papers in your album, keep them simple so the focus remains on the pictures and documents.

Early photographs of my parents offer a glimpse of their lives with family and friends during the 1940s.

First day of school - September, 1958
Beverly, Randy, Dan, and Alice
(Bev was starting first grade)

Waiting for the bus - books are
stacked and lunches are packed -
1966 - Steve, Carol and Lorrie!

May 29, 1958 Last day of School
Dan (7), Randy (6), Alice (9) Kirschner

#10 Bus for New Richmond
Elementary. Dev Kirschner
is sitting next to window
in second seat. About 1963.

First day of school 1962
Barry, Alice, Dan, Randy, Bev
Steve, Carol (starting first
grade at New Richmond)

First day - September, 1962
Boys Only...
Steve, Randy, Dan, Barry
Kirschner

Using one-color die-cuts can liven up black-and-white pictures and pages.

Dogs have always been a big part of our life.
Lori petting Gert and Carol with Queenie's pup - 1964
Gert with two of her pups in the upper right.
Below is Hoss and Carol hugging Hoss in the snow.

I never trust anyone who doesn't have dog hair on their clothes!

Top Left: Queenie and Pup - 1964
Top Right: Mom with Lassie - 1963
Bottom Left: Barry and Alice with Gert - 1955
Bottom Right: Alice + Dan - Gert's pups - 1957

Dogs were always a big part of our family life as children and adults. They were
never just pets; they were always part of the family and included in many of our
photographs year round.

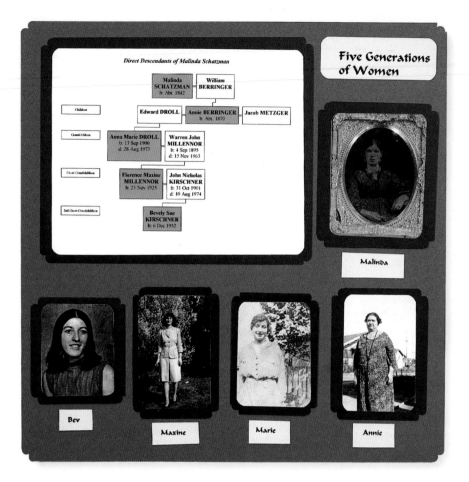

A descendent chart and photographs tie five generations of women together on one page.

Pre-printed papers provide the background for a family tree in your heritage album. Just add the names!

CRAFTING YOUR OWN HERITAGE ALBUM

Cherokee Indians have lived in Cherokee. NC for centuries. Their strong identify with their proud heritage is portrayed in the Oconaluftee Village. Seen here Cherokee woman weave baskets and mold clay into pots. You can learn of the history and culture of the Cherokee people that has been past down from generation to generation.

Authentic Replica of an 18th Century Cherokee Community as it was almost 250 Years ago.

oconaluftee Indian Village Cherokee. NC

Family heritages and traditions should be documented and displayed for future generations.

Family reunion memories are remembered through a newspaper account of the attendees as well as journaling personal recollections.

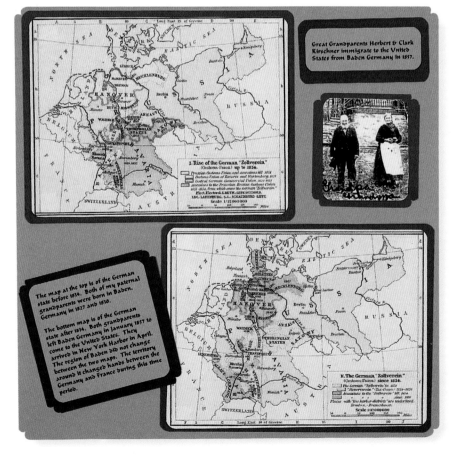

These maps add an historical perspective to the changes in the Eastern European topography during the time my great-grandparents were born and when they later migrated to the United States from Baden, Germany, in the mid-1850s.

BRAUN

The John & Mary Braun Family

Above: In 1963
Dave, Carol, Jerry (front), Tom, Mary, Ted, Bill

Right: 30 Years Later 1993
Bill, Dave, Carol, Mary, Jerry, Ted, Tom

Changes in families are wonderful memories. See the difference between these two
photos taken almost 30 years apart.

We think "Line ups" were Mom and Dad's way of keeping track of all us kids. That was the only way they could tell quickly if someone was missing from the gang.
Top left: Steve, Alice, Bev, Randy Dan & Barry
Top Right: Bev, Pete M, Alice, Karen & Vicki Millennor, Barry, Dan, Randy & Mike Millennor
Left: Steve (in front), Bev, Barry, Dan, Randy, and Alice
Bottom Left: Dad, Barry, Alice, Dan, Randy, Bev, Steve, Carol
Bottom Right: Ronnie, Maria, Bill, Lori, Richard, Rick, Carol, Diane, Diana, Steve – in back: Ethel, Alice, Grandma Marie, Bev

Lining up for photographs made it easier for our parents to tell at a glance if anyone was missing. Mom always had a camera handy, so we have boxes of wonderful old photographs for the heritage album.

Top Left: Alice with Carol, Bev, Dan, Steve, Randy, and Barry in back
Top Right: Dan, Randy, Bev, Barry, Steve hugging Gert, the dog, and Alice
Left: Carol, Steve, Bev, Randy, Dan
Bottom Left: Steve, Bev, Alice, Barry, Dan, Randy
Bottom Right: Dan, Randy, Bev, Steve, Carol

CRAFTING YOUR OWN HERITAGE ALBUM

Exquisite pictures from 1923 and computer journaling celebrate romance and marriage in this elegant two-page layout.

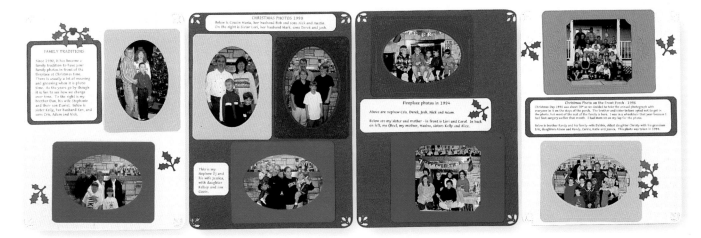

Holiday and family gatherings always include portraits of individual families. These panoramic pages offer extra space and capture the memories of this wonderful tradition.

These pictures were taken at our house on Seymour Avenue in Cincinnati, Ohio in 1952 and 1953.

Top Left: Mom (Maxine Millennor Kirschner) holding Randy, Alice on left, Barry in back, Dan in front.

Middle Left: Randy, Alice, Dan and Bev in 1953.

Bottom Left: Bev in the Taylor Tot. This was an early stroller. The handle and a tray underneath could be removed and it was then used as a walker. This thing lasted forever. This was in 1953.

Above: This is Bev being cooled off in the summer sun. They didn't make kiddie pools in 1953 so Mom improvised. That is Alice, Barry, and Grandma Marie and Grandpa Dusty Millennor in the background.

Early baby pictures are cute but you need to know the story behind the picture to make them an interesting addition to your album. Ask older family members and friends to tell you what they know and include it in your journaling.

Newspaper clippings can provide the basis for documented reminders of good things that can be recorded in your heritage album.

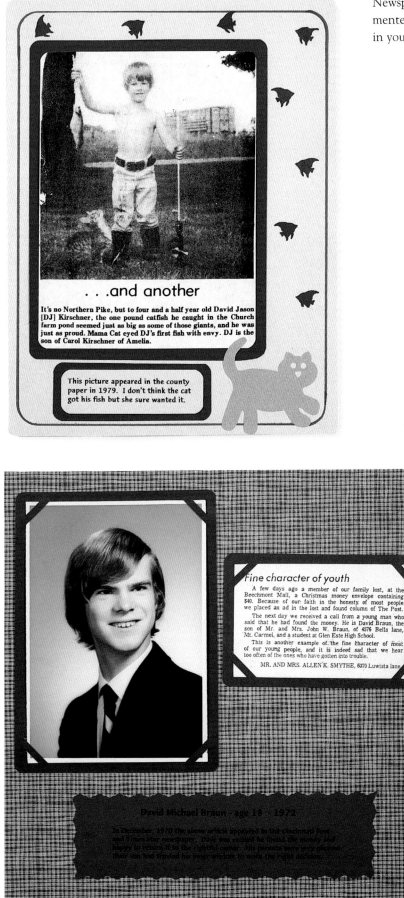

. . .and another

It's no Northern Pike, but to four and a half year old David Jason [DJ] Kirschner, the one pound catfish he caught in the Church farm pond seemed just as big as some of those giants, and he was just as proud. Mama Cat eyed DJ's first fish with envy. DJ is the son of Carol Kirschner of Amelia.

This picture appeared in the county paper in 1979. I don't think the cat got his fish but she sure wanted it.

Fine character of youth

A few days ago a member of our family lost, at the Beechmont Mall, a Christmas money envelope containing $40. Because of our faith in the honesty of most people we placed an ad in the lost and found column of The Post.

The next day we received a call from a young man who said that he had found the money. He is David Braun, the son of Mr. and Mrs. John W. Braun, of 4576 Bells lane, Mt. Carmel, and a student at Glen Este High School.

This is another example of the fine character of most of our young people, and it is indeed sad that we hear too often of the ones who have gotten into trouble.

MR. AND MRS. ALLEN K. SMYTHE, 6070 Luwista lane.

David Michael Braun - age 18 - 1972

In December, 1970 the above article appeared in the Cincinnati Post and Tilton Star newspaper. Dave was excited he found the money and happy to return it to the rightful owner. We were so glad that our son had wanted to learn wisdom to make the right decision.

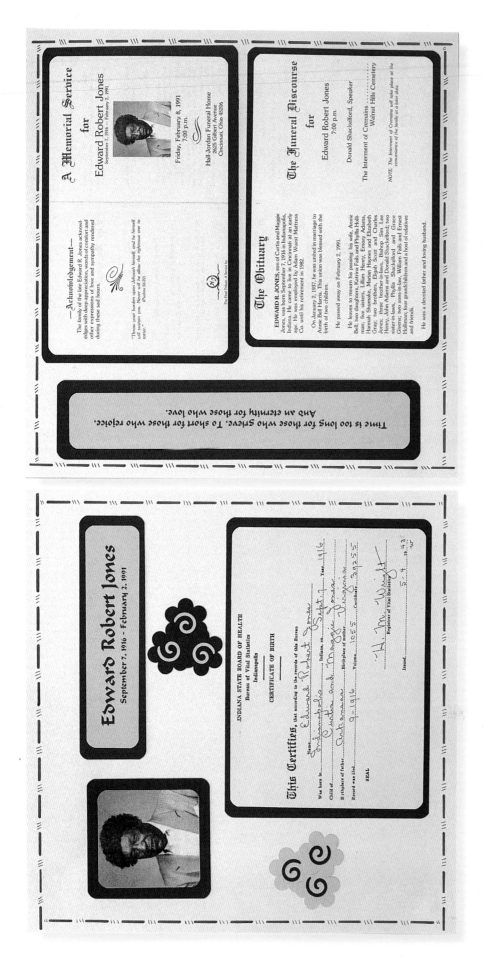

Uncomplicated page layouts displaying a primary birth record document and a secondary memorial card can commemorate a family loved one's life from birth until death.

Lorrie Ann – 1962
age 3¾ – great looking
flower bed!

Bev + Lorrie Kirschner
(age 12½) (age 6½) – 1965

Lorrie Ann practicing
her throwing – 1966
age 8

Lorrie & Carol Kirschner
(age 8) (age 10) 1966

1965 – Lorrie, Mom, and Carol Kirschner

July, 1965 – The Line Up – Cousins, Cousins, Cousins!
Ronnie Millennor, Joey Rossi (almost hidden),
Maria Rossi, Bill Bader, Lorrie Kirschner, Richard Bader,
Rick Rossi, Carol Kirschner, Diane Bader, Diana
Millennor, Steve "Joe" Kirschner – Aunt Ethel (left back),
Alice Marie Kirschner, Grandma Marie Millennor,
Bev Kirschner.

Unadorned black-and-white page layouts with hand journaling may be
added to your heritage album. Even if
you don't know the story behind the
pictures, identify the people in the picture and the time period.

1964
Christmas Day
Morning – Carol and
Lorrie anxiously
await everyone else
to get up and dressed
so presents can be
opened. Notice
the cool boots
Lou has
on.

Christmas
Dinner – 1964
L to R – Bev, Dad, Dan,
Randy, Steve, Lorrie &
part of Mom. Notice the
stack of bread in front of
Mom – she would butter
all the bread and then
deal them out to everyone
around the table like they
were playing cards – and
the bread always landed
butter side up!

Some family traditions would be lost if not documented and
shared. In the bottom photograph is one of these traditions.
My mother would always butter a stack of bread every night
at dinner—one piece for each person at the table (usually
10-12). She would sit at the head of the table and deal the
bread out as if it were a deck of cards. The bread always landed butter-side up next to your plate.

Triple matting in coordinating papers and colors with a pre-embossed frame add a distinctive beauty to this wedding portrait.

Wedding Portrait
Walter Efkeman & Helen Amelia Mummert
11 October 1920 St. Peter & Paul Church, Norwood, Ohio

A descendent chart and the only known photograph of my great-grandparents were the easiest way to document their legacy to my paternal family line.

Direct Descendants of Herbert Kirschner

Herbert Kirschner	Clara Eva Huber
Born: 16 Mar 1827	Born: 24 Mar 1830
Died: 7 Oct 1908	Died: 8 Aug 1921

Joseph Kirschner
Born: 25 Jul 1858
Died: 7 Mar 1863

Anna B. Kirschner
Born: 7 Aug 1861
Died: 13 Jul 1926

Geneova Kirschner
Born: 1863
Died: 7 Jun 1953

Frank Kirschner
Born: 20 Feb 1865
Died: 1 Aug 1900

Barbara Kirschner
Born: 27 Apr 1867
Died: 13 Mar 1954

Nicholas Kirschner
Born: 1 Sep 1869
Died: 7 Jun 1953

Andrew Kirschner
Born: 6 Oct 1872
Died: 25 Oct 1897

This is the only picture I have of my great-great grandparents Herbert and Clara Kirschner.

I think this picture was taken around 1890. Herbert's is about 63 years old and Clara's about 60.

Antique valentines add an elegant touch of romance to these pretty-in-pink album pages.

Mary Jeanette Efkeman 1921-1926

Mary Jeanette Efkeman 1921-22
The very early years!

Top Left: With Grandma Mary Amelia Finke Mummert about age 3 months

Above: Mary at age 3

Bottom Left: Mary at age 5

A mixture of handmade oval frames with corner punched edges and a pre-embossed frame adds a nice focal point to these cute-as-a-button photographs from the early 1920s, taken of my husband's mother.

Mary Jeanette Efkeman
and
William John Braun

50 Years of Marital Bliss
July 17, 1943 - 1993

Two photographs and a journaled nameplate document the subtle changes that occur in a marriage that has lasted more than 55 years.

Early black-and-white page layouts with handwritten journaling of a younger sister were included in her 40th birthday memory album and became part of the family heritage album.

✠ FORMS ✠

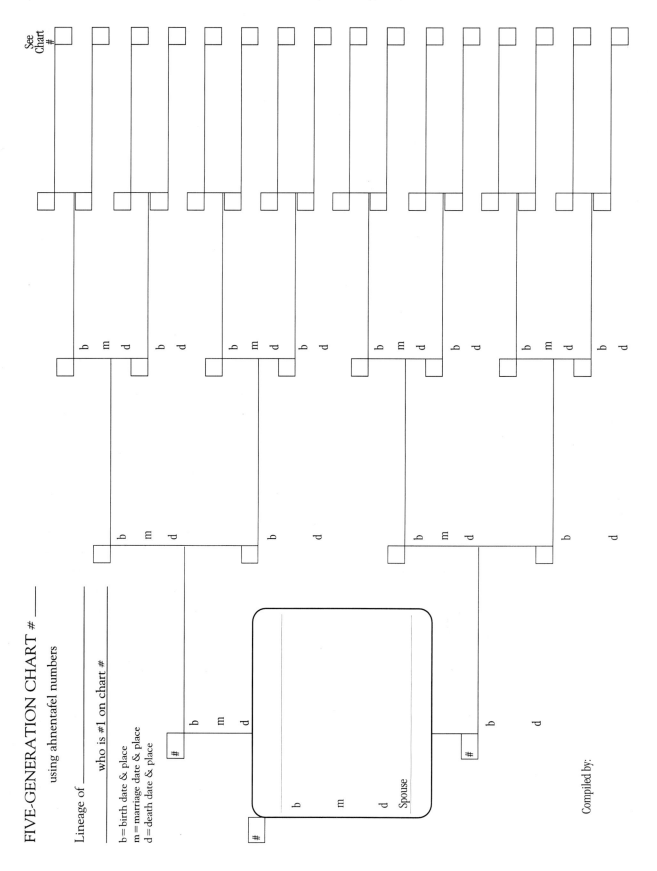

FIVE-GENERATION CHART # _____
using ahnentafel numbers

Lineage of _____
_____ who is #1 on chart # _____

b = birth date & place
m = marriage date & place
d = death date & place

See Chart #

Compiled by:

From *Unpuzzling Your Past Workbook* by Emily Croom

COURTHOUSE RESEARCH LOG

Ancestor's Name:

Objective(s):   Courthouse Name & Location:

Assorted Courthouse Records

Adoptions	Grants	Marriage Records	Subpoena	
Appeals	Tax Lists	Name Changes	Voter Registration	
Autopsy	Divorce Petitions	Naturalization Petition	Wills	
Bankruptcy	Estate Appraisals	Naturalization Decree	Warrants	
Birth Certificates	Guardians	Notice of Sales		
Birth Records	Jury Duty	Notice to Creditors	Other	
Certificate of Freedom	Liens	Notice to Heirs		
Civil Suits	Marriage Applications	Orphan Records		
Death Certificates	Marriage License	Petition to Freedom		
Deeds	Marriage Certificate	Real Estate		

Findings

Date Researched	Volume Number	Record No. & Page No.	Results of Research

Prepared by:

Date:

Family Group Sheet

Husband's Full Name

Information Obtained From:

Date of:	Day Month Year	Town	County	State or Country	Additional Info.
Birth:					
Marriage:					
Death:					
Burial:					
Places of Residence:					
Occupation:		Religion:		Military Record:	
Other wives:					
His father:			His mother:		

Wife's Full Maiden Name

Date of:	Day Month Year	Town	County	State or Country	Additional Info.
Birth:					
Marriage:					
Death:					
Burial:					
Places of Residence:					
Occupation, if other than Housewife:			Religion:		
Other husbands:					
Her father:			Her mother:		

Compiler:

Address:

City:

State:

Date:

Sex:	Children's Full Names:	Date of:	Day Month Year	Town	County	State or Country	Additional Info.
	1.	Birth:					
		Marriage:					
	Full Name of Spouse:	Death:					
		Burial:					
	2.	Birth:					
		Marriage:					
	Full Name of Spouse:	Death:					
		Burial:					
	3.	Birth:					
		Marriage:					
	Full Name of Spouse:	Death:					
		Burial:					
	4.	Birth:					
		Marriage:					
	Full Name of Spouse:	Death:					
		Burial:					
	5.	Birth:					
		Marriage:					
	Full Name of Spouse:	Death:					
		Burial:					
	6.	Birth:					
		Marriage:					
	Full Name of Spouse:	Death:					
		Burial:					
	7.	Birth:					
		Marriage:					
	Full Name of Spouse:	Death:					
		Burial:					
	8.	Birth:					
		Marriage:					
	Full Name of Spouse:	Death:					
		Burial:					

Additional Children

Sex:	Children's Full Names:	Date of:	Day Month Year	Town County State or Country	Additional Info.
	9.	Birth:			
		Marriage:			
	Full Name of Spouse:	Death:			
		Burial:			
	10.	Birth:			
		Marriage:			
	Full Name of Spouse:	Death:			
		Burial:			
	11.	Birth:			
		Marriage:			
	Full Name of Spouse:	Death:			
		Burial:			
	12.	Birth:			
		Marriage:			
	Full Name of Spouse:	Death:			
		Burial:			
	13.	Birth:			
		Marriage:			
	Full Name of Spouse:	Death:			
		Burial:			
	14.	Birth:			
		Marriage:			
	Full Name of Spouse:	Death:			
		Burial:			
	15.	Birth:			
		Marriage:			
	Full Name of Spouse:	Death:			
		Burial:			
	16.	Birth:			
		Marriage:			
	Full Name of Spouse:	Death:			
		Burial:			

Additional Sources

LIBRARY RESEARCH LOG

Ancestor's Name:

Objective(s):

Locality:

DATE	LOCATION/CALL NUMBER	SOURCE DESCRIPTION (Title, Author, Year, Record #, ISBN #)	COMMENTS (Results of Search, Follow-up Required, Names Researched)	Document Number

Prepared by:

Date:

Genealogy Resources

BOOKS

Searching For Your Ancestors: The How and Why of Genealogy

by Gilbert H. Doan and James B. Bell (University of Minnesota Press).

This is the first genealogy book I bought and I still refer to it often. It offers step-by-step guidance to help you construct a family tree, use new computer research methods both in the United States and abroad, trace elusive ancestors and discriminate between promising leads and false information. It includes information that will help you use the Family History Center Library in Salt Lake City, the Library of Congress's Local History and Genealogy Room, the National Archives and regional public libraries.

An Ounce of Prevention: A Guide to the Care of Papers and Photographs

by Craig A. Tuttle (Rainbow Books, Inc.).

This is one of the best books for anyone who collects family photographs, books and documents and needs to know how to care for them. It will also help you determine what type of old photographs you have and what time period they may be from.

Unpuzzling Your Past: A Basic Guide to Genealogy

by Emily Croom (Betterway Books).

This is a great genealogy guide to get you started in genealogical research. In the updated edition, Croom has expanded the chapters on courthouse records, public sources, federal government resources and using computers in genealogy. Includes forms, sample letters and comprehensive resource lists.

The Unpuzzling Your Past Workbook: Essential Forms and Letters for All Genealogists

by Emily Croom (Betterway Books).

This book contains more than 40 forms and letters to help both the novice and experienced researcher to speed the information gathering process. Includes checklists to help you organize your research, guidance on census and military records, and contact logs to make record keeping and presentation easy and fun.

Genealogy On-line for Dummies

by Matthew L. Helm and April Leigh Helm (IDG Books Worldwide).

This is an excellent introductory guide to doing genealogical research on-line. It includes a useful directory to great sites for collecting genealogy information from the WWW, mailing lists, newsgroups and several of the on-line service providers. It explains how to use a home computer to maintain and publish your genealogy information.

The Complete Idiot's Guide to Genealogy

by Christine Rose and Kay Germain Ingalls (Alpha Books).

This book is one of the best guides to genealogy, featuring basic research techniques on how to gather names, dates, places, relationships and family records, along with valuable tips on using genealogy computer programs. It is primarily aimed at the beginner but is also useful as a refresher for those with more experience.

The Internet for Genealogists: A Beginner's Guide

by Barbara Renick and Richard S. Wilson (Compuology).

Completely revised and updated, this guide is a well-written, easy-to-understand beginner's guide to the world of on-line resources for searching your family history on the Internet. It includes more than 200 addresses to genealogy sites, maps, gazetteers, bookstores, libraries and catalogs.

The Genealogist's Companion & Soucebook

by Emily Croom (Betterway Books).

An intermediate-level how-to genealogy book that explains in detail the records that may be found in the various collections and libraries within the United States. It is a companion to Unpuzzling Your Past and does not repeat basic research sources or methods from that book. It also covers government records, cemetery records, newspapers, city directories and African-American and Native American genealogy.

The Handybook for Genealogists

by The Everton Publishers, Inc.

A must-have reference guide for American family historians, especially if you are doing long-distance research. Up-to-date listings of archives, genealogy libraries and societies. State profiles include history and list sources for maps, census and church records. County profiles tell where to find key addresses, property and custody records.

Researching On-line for Dummies

by Reva Basch (IDG Books Worldwide).

This book covers specialty search engines, subject-based catalogs, reference sites, on-line libraries and for-pay information services. It shows you how to think like a researcher—to set goals, determine your strategy and discover new ones along the way. There is a huge difference between "surfing the net" and "searching on-line" and Basch explains the importance of evaluating the information you find to make sure it's relevant and accurate.

First Steps in Genealogy: A Beginner's Guide to Researching Family History by Desmond Allen (Betterway Books). Allen shows you step-by-step how to define your goals and uncover facts about the people behind the names and dates. Offering friendly advice and practical guidance, you'll learn how to organize your research with pedigree charts, family group sheets and filing systems. Includes sample forms, a resource directory and a glossary.

GENEALOGY SOFTWARE

The Family Tree Maker
Broderbund Software Company
Phone: (800) 315-0672
http://www.familytreemaker.com
Available in Windows and Mac formats. I use FTM for my primary genealogy management software and I recommend FTM to newcomers because of its ease of use. FTM has a complete Web site offering on-line classes, Internet Family Finger (your searches locate only genealogical-related information), over 100 CD-ROMs, articles, tips for researching and GenealogyLibrary.com, a subscription service which includes on-line books, databases, family-finding resources and daily updates.

Personal Ancestral File (PAF)
The Church of Jesus Christ of Latter-day Saints (LDS church)
Salt Lake City, Utah
PAF 3.0 and PAF Companion 2.0 (for Windows), which prints reports and charts, is available directly from The Church of Jesus Christ of Latter-day Saints in Salt Lake City Distribution Center for a nominal fee.

Brothers Keeper
John Steed
6907 Childsdale Ave
Rockford, MI 49341
Fax: (616) 866-3345
E-mail: 74774.650@compuserve.com
http://home.sprynet.com/sprynet/steed/

Shareware (not freeware) genealogy program to help you organize your family history information and let you print a large variety of charts and reports. Available for Windows 3.1 and Windows 95/98 or NT. There is no charge to download the trial shareware software, but you must purchase it for $49 if you like it and want to continue using it.

Generation Family Tree from Sierra Family Origins by Broderbund
Broderbund Software Company
Phone: (800) 757-7707
http://www.sierrahome.com
Generations Grande Suite gives you the most complete set of research tools and resources. It has 12 CDs containing 200 million names, access to over 31,000 genealogy Web links, Snapshot SE photo enhancing software, and MasterCook Heritage Edition software. Whether you're just starting to investigate your roots or have been researching them for years, this program offers the easiest way to explore and share your unique heritage.

Ultimate Family Tree
Phone: (800) 548-1806
http://www.uftree.com
Ultimate Family Tree Deluxe offers a broad range of valuable features and time-saving research tools, including Family Tutor, Records Requester, U.S. Gazetteers, an adjustable interface and a free professional genealogy search. It's easy to get started with data entry wizards (PC version only) and Family Tutor, an exclusive multimedia tutorial. Plus, Members Only on-line access to helpful resources and adjustable interface make Deluxe perfect for all users.

RESEARCH FACILITIES AND RESOURCES

National Archives and Records Administration
7th St. and Pennsylvania Ave., NW
Washington, DC 20408

http://www.nara.gov
NARA is an independent federal agency that helps preserve our nation's history by overseeing the management of all federal records. Genealogists are the most numerous users of the Washington, DC research rooms and 13 regional records service facilities of the NARA. It has many records that are useful for genealogical research, such as the federal population census, military service and pension records, immigration records and naturalization records.

Federation of Genealogical Societies
P.O. Box 200940
Austin, TX 78720-0940
Phone: (512) 336-2731
E-mail: fgs-office@fgs.org
Best source to locate a genealogy society in a locale that you are doing research in; sponsors a national conference each year for genealogists of all levels of experience.

MAGAZINES

Ancestry
266 West Center Street
Orem, UT 84057
Phone: (800) 262-3787
http://www.ancestry.com
One of the most informative and authoritative genealogical magazines in the world, this magazine includes articles and columns by some of the best genealogical writers in the field. If you want to keep your genealogical skills sharp, or keep up-to-date with the latest news and techniques, this is a must-have magazine.

Ancestry Genealogical Computing
266 West Center Street
Orem, UT 84057
Phone: (800) 262-3787
http://www.ancestry.com
This is a quarterly magazine geared toward genealogists who use the computer to manage their research and findings. It provides a map to the vast computer resources available for family history. Each issue brings you news

and information about software, CD-ROMs, Internet sites, and how to best use your computer to discover your ancestors.

Everton's Genealogical Helper

P.O. Box 368
Logan, UT 84323-0368
Phone: (800) 443-6325
Fax: (801) 752-0425
http://www.everton.com
One of my personal favorites and the largest genealogical bi-monthly magazine in the world. Offers research articles, "how-to" articles and computer articles for genealogists. Each 300+ page issue is indexed and contains over 150 book reviews.

Canada's Family History News

Family History News c/o Parr's Publishing
525 Ritson Road North
Oshawa, Ontario L1G 5R4 Canada
This quarterly newsletter will help you trace your Canadian ancestry. Provincial reports in each issue cover what is happening and include news from genealogical and family history societies and museums. Some include upcoming historical and genealogical events or seminars that you won't want to miss.

❈ SCRAPBOOK RESOURCES ❈

The Archival Company
P.O. Box 1239
Northampton, MA 01061
Phone: (800) 442-7576 (free catalog)
http://www.archivalcompany.com
museum-quality albums, scrapbooks, storage
boxes, holiday gift ideas

Avery Dennison Consumer Service Center
50 Pointe Drive
Brea, CA 92821
Phone: (800) 462-8379
http://www.avery.com
archival binders, dividers, sheet protectors

Canson-Talens, Inc.
21 Industrial Avenue
South Hadley, MA 01075
Phone: (800) 628-9283
acid-free paper, binders

Century Craft
Phone: (800) 340-2031
archival-quality page protectors

Chatterbox, Inc.
252 Main Street
P.O. Box 216
Star, ID 83669
Phone: (888) 272-3010
E-mail: info@chatterboxpub.com
http://www.chatterboxpub.com
Corner Genies, Journaling Genie templates
and border tools, small books on journaling

Coluzzle Collage Template System
California East, Ltd. 155 Webster St.
Suite M
Hanover, MA 02339-1229
Phone: (781) 982-5515
http://www.coluzzle.com
Coluzzle system (lets you create unique custom collage-puzzles from photographs)

Creative Card Company
1500 West Monroe Street
Chico, IL 60607
Phone: (312) 666-8686
E-mail: ccinquiry@aol.com
embossed photo frames and mattes, archival
paper

Creative Memories
3001 Clearwater Road
P.O. Box 1839
St. Cloud, MN 56302-1839
Phone: (800) 468-9335
http://www.creativememories.com
direct sales through consultants, offering
photo-safe scrapbook albums, accessories

Cut-It-Up
4543 Orange Grove Ave.
Sacramento, CA 95841
Phone: (916) 482-2288
supply totes for all your scrapbooking supplies, Ruler It Up rulers and idea books, creative lettering idea books

Deja Views by C-Thru
6 Britton Dr.
Box 356
Bloomfield, CT 06002
Phone: (860) 243-0303
E-mail: thecrew@cthruruler.com
http://www.cthruruler.com
C-Thru rulers, stencils, templates, edgers,
3D Keepers, acid-free alphabet letters

Donmar Products, Inc.
12784 Perimeter Drive, Suite B-100
Dallas, Texas 75228
Phone: (888) 289-8638
Un-Du Adhesive Remover that temporarily
neutralizes the adhesive on stickers, stamps
and die-cuts so they can be repositioned and
reused

EK Success Ltd.
125 Entin Road
Clifton, NJ 07014
Phone: (201) 939-5404
http://www.eksuccess.com
Zig archival pens and adhesives, Border
Buddy borders, corners and cut-out templates

Family Treasures
24922 Anza Drive Unit A
Valencia, CA 91355-1229
Phone: (800) 413-2645
http://www.familytreasures.com
novelty photo and paper craft supplies—
punches, corner slots, decorative paper scissors in two sizes, albums, stencils, markers,
clip art books, acid-free papers and die-cuts
and light tables

Fiskars, Inc.
P.O. Box 8027
Wausau, WI 54401
Phone: (800) 950-0203
http://www.fiskars.com
paper trimmers, decorative scissors, corner
edgers, rotary cutters, circle cutters

Frances Meyer Inc.
P.O. Box 3088
Savannah, GA 31402
Phone: (800) 372-6237
http://www.francesmeyer.com
Lignin-free and acid-free heritage themed
products, elegant papers, coordinating stickers, alphabet stickers, panoramic page protectors and binders

Highsmith Corruboard Storage & Organization
Phone: (800) 554-4661
inexpensive, acid-free heavy corruboard
storage organizers for photos and supplies

Hiller Photo Albums
631 North 400 West
Salt Lake City, UT 84103
Phone: (801) 521-2411
large selection of photo-safe albums

JM Company
Hasbrouck Heights, NJ 07604
sheet protectors

Keeping Memories Alive
260 N. Main
Spanish Fork, UT 84660
Phone: (800) 419-4949
http://www.scrapbooks.com
Cottage Collection memory papers, acid-free and lignin-free; offers a complete line of the finest preservation materials to make your scrapbooks and memory books fun and exciting

Kodak
Phone: (800) 23Kodak
http://www.kodak.com
film, processing, Kodak picture maker systems for photo duplicating

Leeco Industries
8855 Cypress Woods Dr.
Olive Branch, MS 38654-3805
Phone: (800) 826-8806
E-mail: croperhopr@aol.com
http://www.cropperhopper.com
Cropper Hopper organizers for scrapbook supplies and photo storage

Light Impressions
P.O. Box 940
Rochester, NY 14603-0940
Phone: (800) 828-6216
Fax: (800) 828-5539
E-mail: bsmith@lightimpressionsdirect.com
http://www.lightimpressionsdirect.com/
offers the world's largest variety of fine archival storage, display and presentation materials for negatives, transparencies, CDs, photographs, artwork and documents; sells products to individuals and business

Making Memories
P.O. Box 1188
Centerville, UT 84014
Phone: (800) 286-5263
embossed frames, Creative Letters, Creative Circle Cutter and books

Marco Printed Products Company
Dayton, OH 45458
Phone: (888) 433-5239
http://www.marcopaper.com
archival paper products

Marvy Uchida/Uchida of America Corp.
3535 Del Amo Boulevard
Torrence, CA 90503
Phone: (800) 541-5877
http://www.uchida.com
acid-free markers and matching stamp pads, calligraphy pens

McGill, Inc.
The Craft People
131 E. Prairie St.
Marengo, IL 60152
Phone: (800) 982-9884
paper and border punches

Mrs. Grossman's Paper Company
Box 4467
Petaluma, CA 94955
Phone: (800) 429-4549
http://www.mrsgrossmans.com
acid-free stickers

Olfa Corporation
Osaka, Japan
http://www.olfa.com/olfa/
rotary cutters and mats

Paper Reflections
DMD Industries, Inc.
1205 ESA Drive
Springdale, AR 72764
Phone: (800) 805-9890
http://www.dmdind.com
wheel punches

Pebbles in My Pocket
P.O. Box 1506
Orem, UT 84059-1506
Phone: (800) 438-8153
http://www.pebblesinmypocket.com
on-line store to purchase the newest scrapbooking products (punches, die-cuts, paper, adhesives, pens)

Pioneer Photo Albums
9801 Deering Avenue
P.O. Box 2497
Chatsworth, CA 91313-2497
Phone: (800) 366-3686
http://www.pioneerphotoalbums.com
acid-free memory albums, adhesive mounts, templates

Plaid Enterprises
P.O. Box 7600
Norcross, GA 30091-7600
Phone: (800) 343-3778
Keepsake Keepers (acid-free, archival-safe 3-hole punched memorabilia keepers in two sizes for your scrapbooks for displaying your 2D and 3D treasures)

Preservation Technologies
Phone: (800) 416-2665
Archival Mist de-acidification spray (less than $30)

Print File, Inc.
P.O. Box 607638
Orlando, FL 32860-7638
Phone: (407) 886-3100
E-mail: Support@PrintFile.com
http://www.printfile.com
photographic storage system for negatives, prints, slides and transparencies

Puzzle Mates
Quickcuts
Brea, CA
Phone: (888) 595-2887
E-mail: puzzlemates@aol.com
three puzzle sizes with each template to make quick page layouts with photographs in a variety of shapes.

Sakura of America
30780 San Clemente St.
Hayward, CA 94544
Phone: (510) 475-8880
http://www.gellyroll.com
archival writing instruments (Pigma, Micron, Gelly Rollers, PenTouch Markers)

Shaping Memories
1106 Washington Square
Washington, MO 63090
Phone: (314) 390-8529
http://www.shapingmemories.com
Oval Cropper for cropping photographs and making oval frames in a variety of sizes

Tapestry in Time
1418 Milan Court
Livermore, CA 94550
Phone: (925) 449-3205
http://www.tapestryintime.com
innovative tools for scrapbooking including The Personal Power Punch, The Time Line

Therm O Web
770 Glenn Avenue
Wheeling, IL 60090
Phone: (847) 520-5200
http://www.thermoweb.com
acid-free mounting adhesive

3L Corp.
1120-B Larkin Drive
Wheeling, IL 60090
Phone: (847) 808-1140
adhesives, memorabilia pockets, archival-safe photo corners

Tombow
4467-C Park Drive
Norcross, GA 30093
Phone: (800) 835-3232
http://www.tombow.com
markers, adhesives

Wei T'0 Associates
Phone: (888) 809-3486
Good News line of deacidification sprays and solutions ($20-$38)

RUBBER STAMP RESOURCES

Northwoods Rubber Stamps, Inc.
841 Eagle Ridge Lane
Stillwater, MN 55082
Phone: (612) 430-2840
complete line of rubber stamps and supplies

Rootstamps
6749 White Pine Drive
RR 4 Box 1936
Lakeside, AZ 85929-9431
http://www.whitemtns.com/~roots/
rubber stamps for genealogists, family historians, and scrapbookers; 900+ stamps, pads, punches, scissors, stencils, die-cuts, confetti

Scrapbookin' Stamps for Journaling
3006 S. 363rd Street
Federal Way, WA 98003
Phone: (253) 927-0320
Fax: (253) 927-2559
http://www.scrapbookinstamps.com
over 130 rubber stamps designed specifically to make scrapbook journaling neat, decorative and fun; wholesale and retail catalogs

MAGAZINES

Creating Keepsakes
P.O. Box 1106
Orem, UT 84059-9956
Phone: (888) 247-5282
http://www.creatingkeepsakes.com
Bi-monthly scrapbook magazine filled with layout, lettering, journaling ideas, scrapbook basics, tips and tricks, page makeovers and product reviews.

Memory Makers
475 West 115th Ave. #6
Denver, CO 80234
Phone: (800) 366-6465
Bi-monthly scrapbook magazine that provides ideas and inspiration through scrapbook pages and stories from their readers around the world, who believe in keeping scrapbooks and family photojournalism

alive. Also has a scrapbook idea contest in each edition with cash prizes.

PaperKuts Scrapbook Magazine
P.O. Box 697
Spanish Fork, UT 85660
Phone: (800) 320-0633
Bi-monthly scrapbook magazine with 100+ full-color page layout ideas per issue, with instructions and supply lists for each layout.

Reminisce and Reminisce Extra
Reiman Publications
P.O. Box 5282
Harlan, IA 51593-0782
Phone: (800) 344-6913
www.reimanpub.com
Two separate bi-monthly magazines filled with vintage photographs and stories from the 30s, 40s and 50s. Stories are touching, humorous and provide inspiration for documenting family histories and adding journaling to your pages.

▣ TOP WEB SITES ▣

TOP GENEALOGY WEB SITES

The Church of Jesus Christ of Latter-day Saints Family History Library Records

http://www.familysearch.com

FamilySearch Internet has four types of searches: Ancestor Search, Keyword Search, Custom Search and Browse Categories. It includes the Ancestral File, International Genealogical Index, SourceGuide, Family History Library Catalog and Web sites. The Ancestral File contains over 35 million names organized into families and pedigrees. The International Genealogical Index (IGI) contains over 285 million names extracted from vital records around the world. Thousands of Web sites have been reviewed by the volunteers and categorized to help researchers quickly find relevant family history information. The Web site was new in late spring 1999 and more information becomes available on-line as soon as the records become public.

Cyndi's List of Genealogy Sites on the Internet

http://www.cyndislist.com

Cindi Howell's categorized and cross-referenced index of over 40,000 genealogy sites on the Internet in over 100 categories with links to over 1,000 on-line resources; this is one of the best places to start whether you are a beginner or experienced researcher on the WWW.

Ancestry Hometown

http://www.ancestry.com

Offers one of the largest collections of family history data on-line. New databases and reference materials are added daily to the library to provide the fastest, simplest and most complete resource for family history re-

search. Offers message boards, on-line books, searchable databases, daily and weekly on-line newsletter and how-to articles. Additional services and searchable databases offered for a subscription fee.

Family Tree Maker Online

http://www.familytreemaker.com

Offers on-line classes, Internet Family Finder, over 100 CD-ROMs, articles, tips for researching, and GenealogyLibrary.com, a subscription service which includes on-line books, databases, family finding resources and daily updates.

Everton Publishers

http://www.everton.com

Searchable databases including over 80 million ancestor names, census information, Social Security Death Benefits and linked databases. Searchable message areas offering surname queries, general genealogical questions and research tips; on-line tutorials, on-line resources with links to the genealogy world and on-line chat rooms.

National Archives and Records Administration (NARA)

http://www.nara.gov

NARA is an independent federal agency that helps preserve our nation's history by overseeing the management of all federal records. It contains federal records beginning with the American Revolution and Continental Congress. If ancestors had any dealings with the federal government such as census, immigration or naturalization records, passports, pension records, military, etc, there is a good chance you can find a record of their dealings in the NARA. There are 13 regional records service facilities throughout the United States so you need to check the location of the records

you are searching. Some of the indexes are searchable on-line (census, immigration, naturalization records).

Library of Congress

http://www.loc.gov

The Library provides a variety of services via the Internet, including the library catalog, FTP service, discussion groups and guides to resources on the Internet. The Library serves as a research arm of Congress and is recognized as the national public library of the United States. It offers numerous finding aids and subject bibliographies which describe its holdings.

The National Park Service

http://www.nps.gov

Provides information on all National Parks, as well as historical and educational information, including an on-line bookstore, "this day in history" link and information on collaborative projects involving the NPS with governmental and private organizations and businesses. This is a good place to find information and fill in specific historical details when journaling in your heritage album.

The Journal of On-Line Genealogy

http://www.onlinegenealogy.com

The Journal of On-Line Genealogy (JOG) is to aid the genealogy community in promoting and developing on-line projects, technologies and methods of research. It accomplishes this mission by accepting articles from the genealogy community at large as well as soliciting articles for specific subject matters. The journal is geared for beginning and advanced genealogists around the world who are interested in researching family history through on-line resources.

TOP SCRAPBOOKING WEB SITES

The Scrapbooking Idea Network
http://www.scrapbooking.com
Includes monthly help articles on heritage album topics with "Family Matters." Ideas using die-cuts, border art and lots more.

dMarie
http://www.dmarie.com
Great page layouts—thousands listed by categories; also, a heritage album section, on-line secure shopping and inspiration section with poems, page toppers and a time capsule (historical database of facts from the past to spice up your heritage pages). Also has chat rooms and bulletin boards.

Graceful Bee
http://www.gracfulbee.com
On-line scrapbooking magazine with lots of ideas and inspiration. Regular features on page and album ideas, memory preserving plans and time-saving techniques.

Scrap Happy Scrapbooking
http://www.telepath.com/bcarson/scrap_happy

Jangle
http://www.jangle.com
Includes a live chat room, message boards, news, sayings, retail directory and daily tip section.

ScrapNet
http://www.netprojections.com/scrapnet/scrapnet.htm
Contests, layouts, freebies, new products, clubs, events, pen pals, press releases, swap shop, virtual classes, store directories, clip art, tips, sayings and poetry and more.

Stampin' and Scrappin'
http://www.stampinscrappin.com
On-line catalog and secure on-line shopping and an extremely popular virtual community, message board, convention news, tips and ideas, retail store locator and rubber stamp cards.

The Cropping Corner
http://www.croppingcorner.com
Page layout ideas categorized by themes, products and on-line shopping, tips and ideas.

The Scrapbook Obsession
http://www.geocities.com/Heartland/Ranch/2637/
Includes tip of the month, layouts, poem of the month, chat rooms, message boards, and on-line greeting cards you can send to scrapbooking friends.

Clarke Historical Library Preservation
http://www.lib.cmich.edu/clarke/pres.htm
Designed to help individuals better care for the things that preserve their memories, including information on how to find and use archival-quality supplies for your scrapbook and memory book projects. Also, how to care for letters, diaries, books and other paper memories.

GLOSSARY

abstract
Summary of a document that maintains every pertinent detail.

acid-free
Materials that have a pH of 7.0 or higher. This term indicates the absence of acid; acid can quickly break down paper and photographs. This term is sometimes used incorrectly as a synonym for alkaline or buffered.

acid migration
The transfer of acid from an acidic material to a less acidic material or pH-neutral material. Acid always migrates to neutral, never the other way around.

archival quality
Term indicating a material or product is permanent, durable or chemically stable, and that it can, therefore, safely be used for preservation.

buffered paper
A paper that is pH neutral to begin with, and has been made more alkaline to neutralize additional acids that may migrate to the paper.

citation
Form notation of the source from which the information was taken. In genealogy research, each fact needs at least one citation.

lignin
Largely responsible for the strength and rigidity of plants. Its presence in paper is believed to contribute to chemical deterioration. Paper with less than one percent lignin is considered lignin-free. Lignin is believed to be more harmful to photos than acid.

Mylar (polyester, polypropylene)
Used as a protective clear covering for photos and album pages. Mylar is currently regarded as the highest quality material used for this purpose.

photo-safe
A term loosely used by many companies to indicate they believe their products are safe to use with photographs. There is no regulation of this term by a legally enforceable standard. This term is used in many instances when a product is not safe to be used near photos.

polyvinyl chloride (PVC)
A substance found in some plastic products and adhesives that can break down to form acids.

INTERNET JARGON

browser
Short for Web browser. It's the tool that allows you to surf the Web. The most popular Web browsers right now are Netscape Navigator and Internet Explorer.

cyberspace
Term used to describe the Internet.

E-mail (electronic-mail)
Electronic messages sent from one person to another over the Internet.

FAQ
Acronym for Frequently Asked Questions.

forum
An electronic meeting place where messages can be exchanged.

GEDCOM
A standard file format used for exchanging data between different genealogy databases and programs.

HTML
Hypertext Mark-up Language. HTML is not really a programming language, but a way to format text by placing marks around the text. HTML is the basis for most Web pages.

http
Hypertext Transfer Protocol. A protocol that tells computers how to communicate with each other. Most Web page locations begin with "http://".

Internet
A system of computer networks joined together by high-speed data lines called backbones.

ISP
Internet Service Provider. This is your connection to the Internet. You use an ISP to connect onto the Internet every time you log on. The most popular ISPs are America Online, Prodigy and CompuServ.

Link
A link will transport you from one Internet site to another with just a click of the mouse. Links can be text or graphic.

Location
An Internet address.

Modem
Allows computers to transmit information to one another over an ordinary telephone line.

Net
Short for Internet.

On-line
Having access to the Internet.

Personal Web Page
A page on the World Wide Web
that was designed and posted by
an individual or family.

Site
A place on the Internet. Every Web
page has a location where it resides,
which is called its site. Every site has
an address usually beginning with
"http://".

URL
An acronym for Uniform Resource
Locator. It is the address of each
Web site. It usually begins with
"http://".

WWW
An acronym for the World Wide
Web.

Web
Short for World Wide Web.

Web Browser
The tool (or program) that allows you to surf
the Web.

Web Page
Also called a home page; a multimedia document that is created in HTML and view-
able on the Internet with the use of a
browser.

World Wide Web
A full-color, multimedia database
of information on the Internet.
Like the name implies, the World
Wide Web is a universal mass of
Web pages connected together
through links.

❖ Index ❖